The Grammar of the Gods

Archetypes, Myth, and the Structure of the Unconscious

Gonzalo Esteban Meza

DEDICATION

To my father, **José Esteban Meza**, the archetypal Engineer. You taught me the Cartesian architecture of reality, the quiet power of mathematics, and the rigor of the scientific method. You gave me the map.

To my mother, **Gladys Haydée Secco**, who taught me that the map is not the territory. You showed me that there is always more than meets the eye, revealing the power of the Letter and the sacred necessity of human connection. You gave me the mystery.

And to my wife, **Gülşah Meza**. My Muse, my witness, and my partner in the Great Work. You show me, every single day, that the adventure is worth the risk. Thank you for walking this path of individuation by my side—holding the sacred tension of the "right distance," close enough to love, yet far enough to be free.

"Love consists in this, that two solitudes protect and touch and greet each other."
Rainer Maria Rilke

Copy Editing & Proofreading: Gulsah Meza

Published by: Alpha Self Publishing Printed by: XXXX

ISBN: 978-2-488936-00-2

Legal Deposit: January 2026

INDEX

ACKNOWLEDGEMENTS

My deepest gratitude goes to the lights that have guided me through the dark.

To **Gülsah**, my partner in every sense. You are the stillness in my storm and the wind in my sails. Thank you for the endless gifts of your presence. Life with you is the greatest story I know.

To the silent current that runs beneath the surface of the Ego - whether we call it the Unconscious, the Universe, or Grace. Thank you for the synchronicities that were never truly coincidences, but the meaningful alignment of our inner and outer worlds, waiting for us to become conscious of them.

And to every soul I have met along the way. Whether you brought kindness or challenge, you helped carve the shape of who I have become. Every interaction was a necessary step on the stair.

As Rumi reminds us: *"The wound is the place where the Light enters you."*

INTRODUCTION: THE MAP OF THE SKY IS A MAP OF THE SOUL

I. The Mirror in the Dark

There is a moment, perhaps one you have felt, when you step out of your house on a winter night. You move away from the glare of streetlights and the distraction of screens to look up. For a second, the familiar world of deadlines, debts, and dinner plans vanishes. You are confronted with the crushing, silent majesty of the dark.

In that silence, two things happen simultaneously. The first is a sense of absolute insignificance. You are a speck of dust on a rock drifting through an infinite void. The second is a paradoxical sense of profound connection. You feel in your bones that the vastness "out there" is somehow answering a vastness "in here." You are not merely observing the universe; you are recognizing it. You feel a resonance that predates memory. The very atoms composing your hands, your eyes, and your heart were not created here. They were forged in the nuclear kilns of dying stars billions of years ago. You are, quite literally, the debris of a supernova gathered by gravity and time into a feeling, thinking form. The iron in your blood is a stellar inheritance; the carbon in your breath is cosmic dust. You share this source and this same ancient matter with the rest of the Solar System.

For thousands of years, human beings did not look up at the sky and see balls of gas or chunks of frozen methane. They saw gods. They saw the writers of destiny. They saw a great cosmic script in which their own lives were merely a single sentence. When the ancients looked at the red wanderer, Mars, they did not see iron oxide. They felt the surge of adrenaline, the heat of anger, the metallic taste of blood, and the courage to defend a boundary. When they looked at the golden glow of Venus, they did not see a toxic atmosphere of sulfuric acid. They felt the pull of attraction, the softening of the heart, and the terrifying vulnerability of love.

They understood something that we, in our age of high-definition telescopes and spectral analysis, have largely forgotten: the map of the sky is the map of the soul.

This work serves as a journey of remembrance. It is an expedition to reclaim the solar system not as a collection of physical objects, but as a collection of psychological realities. We travel from the ego-centric fire of the Sun to the dissolving mists of Neptune, and down into the underworld of Pluto. But we are not traveling through space. We are traveling through the layers of your own mind.

The premise here is built upon the ancient Hermetic maxim *Quod est superius est sicut quod inferius*, which translates to "As above, so below." This is not a magical claim that the position of Jupiter at the moment of your birth literally forces you to be generous or lucky. It is a psychological truth. The universe we perceive is the universe we are capable of perceiving. The structures we see outside are reflections of the structures that exist inside. The "gods" of the ancients were not hallucinations; they were projections. They were the externalized names for the internal forces that drive, torment, and inspire us.

We live in a time of fragmentation. We have separated science from myth, fact from meaning, and the outer world from the inner world. The result is a peculiar form of modern loneliness. We know exactly how much Saturn weighs (5.683 × 10^26 kg), but we have forgotten what Saturn *means*. We have lost touch with the Saturn within us, that part of our psyche which understands limits, respects time, and builds enduring structures. Without a relationship to these archetypal forces, we are left at their mercy. We do not stop being influenced by Mars just because we stop believing in him. We simply call it "stress," or "rage issues," or "burnout." We take a pill, or two, or choose to medicate ourselves with the Maenad’s Prescription. We do our best to continue as if nothing has happened until we simply can’t anymore.

Furthermore, we live in a culture of aggressive superficiality. We are inundated with thirty-second videos that either anesthetize the mind or offer dangerously simple solutions to complex problems. We are told that if we simply place a blue crystal on the fifth chakra, our childhood traumas will magically evaporate. We are assured that repeating a specific affirmation three times a day will effortlessly manifest a seven-figure income. But the soul cannot be hacked. It does not respond to life-hacks or quick fixes. The psyche is deep, slow, and geological; it requires a different kind of attention, one that resists the temptation of the easy answer. This work demands effort and time; to claim otherwise is to gaslight the soul, to deny its very essence.

These pages attempt to heal that split. They act as a guide to the inner solar system. By exploring the myths and stories associated with these eleven celestial bodies, we uncover the architecture of the human psyche. We use the telescope of psychology to look at the stars, and the mirror of mythology to look at ourselves.

II. The Council of Gods

The human psyche is not a unity. It is a multiplicity.

For centuries, Western culture has been dominated by monotheism: the idea of one God, one Truth, one Way. This theological preference has seeped into our psychology. We like to believe that we are "one person," ruled by a single, rational decision-maker called "I." We imagine this "I" sits in the control room of the brain, looking at screens, pulling levers, and steering the ship of our life in a straight line.

But anyone who has ever tried to stick to a diet, save money, or keep a New Year's resolution knows that this is a lie.

You decide to save money (Saturn), but then you see a beautiful object and buy it on impulse (Venus). You decide to remain calm at work (Sun), but someone insults you and you suddenly explode in fury (Mars). You decide to be productive (Mercury), but you find yourself staring out the window, lost in a daydream for hours (Neptune).

Who are these people? Who is the "I" that buys the object, and who is the "I" that regrets it?

The Swiss psychiatrist Carl Jung suggested that the psyche is not a monarchy; it is an oligarchy. It is inhabited by *archetypes*, those universal, primordial patterns of behavior and instinct. These archetypes are the "organs" of the soul. Just as your body has a heart to pump blood and a stomach to digest food, your psyche has a Mars to fight battles and a Venus to form bonds. These forces are autonomous. They have their own wills, their own desires, and their own logic.

In the ancient world, this psychological reality was understood as Polytheism. A Greek citizen knew that life was a negotiation between competing powers. You could not worship Artemis (chastity and the hunt) and Aphrodite (erotic love) in the same breath. You had to honor both, but you understood they were different domains. If you neglected one god for too long, that god would take revenge. If you ignored Aphrodite, your life would become dry, joyless, and brittle. If you ignored Mars, you would become weak and unable to defend yourself.

In modern psychology, we call this "neurosis." A neurosis is often nothing more than a god who has been ignored. It is an archetype or a fundamental necessity that has been repressed into the unconscious. There it festers and grows toxic, eventually erupting in symptoms, anxiety, or self-sabotage.

This book views the solar system as a "Council of Gods." Each planet represents a seat at the table of your inner life.

- **The Sun** is the Ego, the Chairman of the Board, trying to maintain order.
- **The Moon** is the emotional body, the memory, the gut instinct.
- **Mercury** is the intellect, the data analyst, the communicator.
- **Venus** is the drive for union, beauty, and value.
- **Mars** is the drive for separation, aggression, and agency.
- **Jupiter** is the principle of expansion, growth, and hope.
- **Saturn** is the principle of contraction, discipline, and reality.
- **Uranus** is the revolutionary, the breaker of chains, the flash of insight.
- **Neptune** is the mystic, the dreamer, the dissolver of boundaries.
- **Pluto** is the transformer, the lord of death and rebirth.
- **Earth** is the ground of reality, the place where all these energies must be materialized.

A healthy psyche is not one where the "I" has crushed all opposition. That is the path of repression and rigidity. A healthy psyche is a democracy. It is a state where the Ego (the Sun) is strong enough to hold the center, but wise enough to listen to the voices of the council, to value their contributions and honor their needs. It is a state where Mars is allowed to fight for what is right, but not allowed to start a war in the living room; where Saturn is allowed to set a budget, but not allowed to starve the joy out of life.

Our goal in these chapters is to introduce you to your council members. Some of them you may know well. Some of them may be strangers to you. Some of them may be strangers to you. Some of them you may fear. But they are all *you*. And until you can hear their voices, you cannot conduct the music of your own life.

III. The Architecture of Desire

If Carl Jung provides us with the map of the territory, comprising the images and the archetypes, it is the French psychoanalyst Jacques Lacan who provides us with the structural mechanics of the vehicle.

While Jung looks at the *content* of the psyche (the stories, the images), Lacan looks at the *structure* of desire. He asks: Why do we want what we want? Why is satisfaction always just out of reach? How does language shape our reality?

In this exploration, we use Lacanian concepts as a secondary lens to sharpen our understanding of the planetary forces. Specifically, we see how the planets operate within the three registers of human experience: the Imaginary, the Symbolic, and the Real.

The Imaginary is the realm of images, mirrors, and wholeness. It is the domain of **Venus** and the **Moon**. It is where we fall in love with an image of ourselves or another. It is the place of wholeness and capture, but also of illusion. When we look at the Moon, we are looking at the Mirror Stage where we recognize ourselves and simultaneously become alienated from ourselves.

The Symbolic is the realm of language, law, and social structure. It is the domain of **Saturn**, **Jupiter**, and **Mercury**. It is the world of rules, names, titles, and "The Father." It is the structure that allows civilization to exist, but it comes at a cost. To enter the Symbolic, we must sacrifice our primal, unbridled enjoyment. Saturn is the gatekeeper of this realm, the stern father who says "No" and in doing so creates the structure of desire.

The Real is the realm of the unrepresentable. It is that which cannot be spoken, categorized, or tamed. It is the raw intensity of existence before we put a name on it. It is the domain of **Uranus**, **Neptune**, and **Pluto**. The Real is the trauma that disrupts our smooth lives. It is the earthquake, the orgasm, the moment of death, the flash of madness. It is the chaotic ocean of Neptune and the volcanic fire of Pluto.

Understanding these registers is crucial because the planets often represent the tension between them. **Mars**, for instance, is the drive (Trieb) that constantly circles the object of desire but never quite captures it. **Mercury** is the "sliding signifier," the word that changes meaning, the trickster who reveals that language is slippery.

Lacan teaches us that the human subject is defined by a fundamental "lack." We are born prematurely, helpless, and we spend the rest of our lives trying to fill the hole in our being. We try to fill it with love (Venus), with power (Mars), with knowledge (Mercury), with status (Jupiter). But the hole is structural. It cannot be filled.

This sounds depressing, but it is actually the engine of life. It is this lack that causes us to move, to create, to build, to love. If we were complete, we would be stones. Because we are incomplete, we are seekers.

The planets describe the different ways we navigate this lack. **Jupiter** tries to fill it with *more*: more land, more wisdom, more God. **Saturn** tries to manage the lack by building walls around it. **Neptune** tries to deny the lack by dissolving into the infinite. **Pluto** forces us to face the lack, to enter the void and realize that there is nothing to fear.

By weaving Jung's rich imagery with Lacan's structural rigor, we aim to provide a comprehensive view of the soul that honors both the beauty of the myth and the brutal reality of the mechanism.

IV. The Vehicle of Myth

Why myths? Why are we using stories about Sumerian goddesses, Norse wolves, and Japanese moon-princesses to understand modern psychology? Why not just use clinical case studies or neurological data?

We use myths because the unconscious mind does not speak English. It does not speak French or German or Spanish. It speaks *Image*. It speaks *Story*.

When you dream, your brain does not send you a text message saying, "You are feeling anxious about your upcoming presentation." It sends you a dream where you are naked in a classroom and your teeth are falling out. The unconscious communicates in symbols, metaphors, and narratives.

Therefore, if we want to communicate *with* the unconscious, if we want to effect real change in the psyche, we must speak its language. Logical explanations are useful for the ego, but they rarely penetrate the deeper layers of the mind. You can intellectually understand that you shouldn't be afraid of intimacy, but that understanding rarely stops the fear. To change the feeling, you need a story.

This book is written using a specific narrative technology. In the "Context" sections, we speak to your intellect, giving you the history and the rationale. But in the "Myth" sections, we speak to your unconscious.

These retellings utilize patterns drawn from Ericksonian hypnosis. You may notice shifts in tense, embedded commands, sensory-rich descriptions, and rhythmic pacing. This is intentional. The goal is to induce a state of light trance to soften the critical faculty. We want to bypass the bouncer at the door of your mind and smuggle the archetype directly into the VIP section.

When we tell the story of **Inanna descending into the underworld**, we don't want you to merely *analyze* Inanna. We want you to *walk with her*. We want you to feel the dust on your skin, the weight of the heavy jewelry, and the humiliation of being stripped naked at the seven gates. We want you to experience the surrender of the ego, not just think about it.

Myths are not lies. They are, as the mythologist Joseph Campbell said, "public dreams." They are the collective dreams of the human species. They have survived for thousands of years not because they are factually true, but because they are psychologically true. They are the source code of human behavior.

By engaging with these stories, we are performing a kind of software update on our own minds. We are refreshing our connection to the source. We are reminding the psyche of the pathways that have been laid down by millions of ancestors before us.

V. The Itinerary

Our journey takes us through eleven stations, spiraling out from the center and then returning to the ground beneath our feet.

1. The Sun: The Hero and the Ego We begin in the blinding center. The Sun is the archetype of the Hero, the Father, and the conscious Ego. We travel to ancient Egypt to witness the nightly battle of the sun god **Ra** against the serpent **Apophis**. Here, we learn that consciousness is not a permanent state of victory, but a cyclical maintenance task. The Ego must constantly defend itself against the entropy of the unconscious. We explore the necessity of the Hero as well as the arrogance of the Sun, specifically the danger of believing that "I" am the center of the universe.

2. The Moon: The Reflection and the Unconscious From the fire of the Sun, we move to the cool reflection of the Moon. This is the realm of the Anima, the Mother, and memory. We listen to the Japanese tale of **Kaguya-hime**, the Bamboo Cutter's daughter. Through her story, we examine the nature of longing and the Lacanian mirror. The Moon teaches us about the things we can see but cannot touch, the impossible objects of desire that structure our emotional lives. We confront the pain of separation and the beauty of the reflected light.

3. Mercury: The Trickster and the Word Next, we meet the quicksilver messenger. Mercury is the god of the intellect, the boundary-crosser, the Trickster. We travel to the Gran Chaco of South America to follow the cycle of **Tokjuaj**, the trickster spirit. Mercury teaches us about the slipperiness of language. He shows us that words are not stable containers of truth, but sliding signifiers that are constantly evading our grasp. We learn how the intellect can be a tool for connection or a weapon of deception.

4. Venus: Eros and the Object of Desire We then enter the garden of Venus. This is the archetype of Union, Value, and Aesthetics. We retell the classic myth of **Psyche and Eros**, a story that maps the difficult journey of integrating the feminine and the masculine principles. Venus is not just about "love" in the romantic sense; it is about *valuation.* It is about what we find beautiful and worth pursuing. We explore the Lacanian concept of *objet petit a.* This is the little object of desire that causes us to run, the missing piece that we think will make us whole.

5. Mars: The Warrior and the Drive Leaving the garden, we step onto the battlefield. Mars is the archetype of Separation, Willpower, and Aggression. We look to the Norse myth of **Tyr and Fenrir**, where the god of war must sacrifice his hand to bind the chaotic wolf. This chapter confronts the shadow of violence and the necessity of courage. We distinguish between destructive rage and the holy anger that protects life. We look at the concept of Drive, that relentless energy that circles the object but never lands.

6. Jupiter: The King and Expansion From the soldier, we turn to the King. Jupiter is the principle of Expansion, Meaning, and the Benevolent Father. We ride with the **Legend of Oghuz Khagan** from the Turkic steppes. Jupiter represents the "Mana Personality," representing the larger-than-life energy that establishes the law and expands the territory. We look at how we create meaning, how we establish the Symbolic Order, and the dangers of inflation where we become so big that we lose touch with the ground.

7. Saturn: The Senex and the Limit Every expansion meets a boundary. Saturn is the archetype of Time, Structure, and the Wise Old Man. We witness the terrifying Greek myth of **Cronus devouring his children**. Saturn is the hardest teacher. He brings depression, limitation, and death. But he also brings mastery. We explore the "Saturnian Shadow" and the Superego, that voice in the head that judges and restricts. We learn that without Saturn's walls, Jupiter's roof would collapse.

8. Uranus: The Awakener and Rebellion Suddenly, lightning strikes. Uranus is the archetype of Rebellion, Insight, and the shattering of the status quo. We recount the theft of fire by **Prometheus**. Uranus represents the trauma of the Real, which is the sudden event that ruptures our symbolic world. It is the divorce, the accident, the epiphany. We explore the necessity of breaking the persona to find the true self, and the dangerous electricity of evolution.

9. Neptune: The Mystic and Dissolution The lightning fades into the mist. Neptune is the Dreamer, the Mystic, and the Illusionist. We descend into the waters with the Mapuche legend of **Tren Tren and Kai Kai Vilu**, the serpents of earth and sea. Neptune dissolves the boundaries that Saturn built. It is the realm of spirituality, addiction, and madness. We look at the "Oceanic Feeling," defined as the desire to return to the womb of the universe, and the fine line between the mystic and the psychotic.

10. Pluto: Death and Rebirth We reach the bottom of the well. Pluto is the Lord of the Underworld, the archetype of Transformation and Power. We walk the path of **Inanna** as she descends to meet her dark sister, Ereshkigal. Pluto demands the death of the ego. It is the "subjective destitution." This process involves the stripping away of all identifiers until only the naked soul remains. We learn that the gold we seek is hidden in the darkest place, and that the only way out is through.

11. Earth: The Mother and Reality Finally, we return home. Earth is not usually included in astrological textbooks, which is a tragedy of omission. Earth is the stage where the drama plays out. It is the Archetype of Substance and Incarnation. We tell the folktale of **The Smith and the Devil**. Earth teaches us about the *Sinthome*, the art of using our craft, our work, and our reality to bind the chaotic forces of the Real. It is here that we take the lessons of the sky and hammer them into a life worth living.

VI. The Conductor's Baton

This book is structured as a hologram. Each chapter stands alone, yet each contains the reflection of the others. You do not need to read them in order, though the sequence follows a logic of deepening descent and return.

As you read, pay attention to which chapters repel you and which ones attract you. If you find yourself bored by **Saturn**, ask yourself: Where in my life am I refusing to grow up? Where am I resisting structure? If you find yourself disgusted by **Mars**, ask yourself: Where have I disowned my own power? Where am I being too passive? Or alternatively, what part of my own aggression do I see reflected in this archetype? If you are seduced by **Neptune**, ask yourself: What am I trying to escape?

The psychological mechanism at play here is *resonance*. The archetypes within you will vibrate in sympathy with the stories on the page. When you feel that vibration, be it excitement, fear, anger, or grief, stop. Put the book down. That is the work. That is the god knocking on the door.

We are not attempting to "fix" you. The goal of this book is not self-improvement in the sense of becoming a more productive worker or a happier consumer. The goal is *wholeness.*

Wholeness does not mean perfection. It means integration. It means knowing that you contain a murderer (Mars), a saint (Neptune), a miser (Saturn), and a whore (Venus), and being able to sit at the head of the table and facilitate the conversation between them.

The modern world often demands that we be one thing: consistent. We are expected to have one career, one personality, one brand. But the soul is not consistent. It is a weather system. It contains storms and droughts, heat waves and freezes.

When we deny this complexity, we become flat. We become two-dimensional caricatures of human beings. We project our disowned gods onto others. We hate the "aggressive" politician because we have disowned our Mars just as we envy the "free" artist because we have disowned our Uranus.

By reclaiming these projections, we take back our energy. We take back our gold.

This journey requires courage. It is not easy to look at the Medusa of your own envy, or the Minotaur of your own lust. But it is the only journey that matters. It is the journey from being a victim of fate to being a collaborator with destiny.

In the final analysis, the planets are not masters to be served, nor are they enemies to be conquered. They are instruments. You are the orchestra. For too long, perhaps, the brass section has been drowning out the strings, or the percussion has been asleep. The music has been discordant, repetitive, or faint.

But the conductor is stepping up to the podium. The baton is raised. The silence before the downbeat is heavy with potential.

It is time to play.

Welcome to *The Planets.*

A Note on the Text

Throughout this book, you will encounter terms from the Analytical Psychology of C.G. Jung and the Psychoanalysis of Jacques Lacan. We have done our best to define these terms within the flow of the narrative. However, for those who wish for a more precise definition, a Glossary is provided at the back of the book.

You will also notice a shift in tone between the "Context," "Myth," and "Reflection" sections of each chapter. The "Myth" sections are written to be read slowly, perhaps even aloud. They are designed to be felt rather than analyzed. We encourage you to allow the images to wash over you without immediately trying to dissect them. There is plenty of time for dissection in the "Reflection" that follows.

For now, simply trust the story. The story, and your psyche, know the way.

1 THE SUN: THE HERO'S JOURNEY AND THE EGO

Archetype: The Center, Consciousness, The Hero, The Father
Myth: Ra and the Serpent Apophis

I. The Context: The Solar Barque and the Architecture of Night

In the vast, golden theology of Ancient Egypt, the sun was not a static object of physics, but a dynamic subject of drama. To the priests of Heliopolis, the sun god **Ra** was the ultimate affirmation of life. He was the *Khepri* (the scarab beetle) at dawn, the self-created one who pushes the ball of the sun above the horizon. He was *Ra-Horakhty* at noon, the falcon soaring at the zenith of visibility and power. And he was *Atum* at dusk, the weary old man sinking into the west (Assmann 2001).

But the most critical part of Ra's existence, and the part most relevant to our psychological study, was not his glorious transit across the day-sky, but his terrifying voyage through the night.

The Egyptians believed that when the sun set, it did not merely disappear; it entered a different dimension entirely: the **Duat**, or the Underworld. This was not a "hell" in the Christian sense of a place of punishment, but rather a womb of regeneration, a chaotic, magical realm where the laws of physics were suspended. To rise again in the east, Ra had to traverse the twelve hours of the night, sailing his night-barque, the *Mesektet*, through a river of darkness that wound its way through the corpse of the earth (Hornung 1999).

This journey was described in intricate detail in the *Amduat* ("The Book of What is in the Underworld"), a funerary text reserved for pharaohs. The text describes a harrowing gauntlet. In each hour, Ra faces different demons, gates, and trials. He must speak the names of the gatekeepers to pass; he must bring light to the blessed dead who reside on the riverbanks; he must regenerate his own aging body, merging with the corpse of Osiris to find new life (Faulkner 1972).

However, the climax of this journey, occurring roughly at the seventh hour (the deepest part of the night), was the encounter with **Apophis** (known in Egyptian as *Apep*).

Apophis was not a god. In the Egyptian pantheon, gods (Neteru) represent functions of nature and order (*Ma'at*). Apophis represented *Isfet* - chaos, uncreation, and the void. He was a colossal serpent, said to be thousands of cubits long, whose roar could shake the underworld. He did not want to rule the world; he wanted to dissolve it. His goal was to swallow the Solar Barque whole, stopping the passage of time and returning the cosmos to the *Nun* - the inert, primeval waters that existed before creation.

If Apophis won, the sun would not rise. Time would stop. The heartbeat of the universe would fail.

The central paradox of this myth, and the key to our chapter, is Ra's defense. Ra, the embodiment of light, order, and kingship, is oddly passive during this encounter. He is often depicted as protected by a coil of the friendly serpent Mehen or simply standing as the source of light. He cannot defeat Apophis himself. Light cannot destroy darkness; it can only illuminate it. To destroy the monster that seeks to unmake the world, Ra requires a champion who possesses a nature close to the monster itself.

He requires **Set**.

Set is the black sheep of the Egyptian pantheon. He is the god of the red desert, of storms, of violence, of foreigners, and of confusion. He is the one who, in the famous Osiris myth, murders his brother Osiris out of jealousy and hacks his body into pieces. He is often seen as a villain, a usurper, a force of disruption. Yet, every night, on the prow of the *Mesektet*, Set is the hero. He is the only god strong enough to look Apophis in the eye without being hypnotized. He is the only one who possesses the raw, aggressive violence necessary to drive a spear into the serpent's neck and turn the boat back toward the dawn (Te Velde 1967).

This creates a complex psychological image: The God of Order (Ra) survives only because he is guarded by the God of Chaos (Set). The Ego survives the Night only because it employs the Shadow.

II. The Myth

Take a moment to adjust your position, allowing your spine to rest against the support behind you. Let your hands fall loosely into your lap, or by your sides, heavy and still. There is nothing you need to do right now. The demands of the day, the lists of tasks, the voices of the outer world - they can all wait outside the door. For now, there is only the rhythm of your breath. In... and out.

As you watch your breath, you might notice that the light in the room seems to be changing. It is not getting darker, exactly, but the quality of the light is shifting. It is becoming older. It is the color of sand at twilight. The color of dried papyrus. And as you breathe out, you feel the ground beneath you dissolving, turning into the gentle, rocking motion of a boat.

You are no longer in the room. You are standing on the deck of a great vessel, the Mesektet. The wood beneath your bare feet is ancient cedar, polished smooth by eons of travel, warm and vibrating with a low, humming energy. Above you, there is no sky, only a cavernous, overarching darkness, heavy and silent like the inside of a mountain. You are traveling through the veins of the earth.

The river you sail upon is not water. It is a sleek, obsidian substance, thicker than water, silent as oil. It reflects nothing. No stars. No moon. Only the faint, golden glow that emanates from the center of the boat.

There, in the midst of the deck, stands the shrine. Inside it rests the Flesh of Ra. He appears as an old man, his skin etched with the cracks of a million years, his body huddled and small. He is asleep. This is the consciousness of the world, tired, withdrawn, vulnerable. He is dreaming the world into existence, but his dream is fragile. If he wakes in terror, the world ends. If he dies, the world vanishes.

You look around the boat. There are other figures here: strange, silent deities with the heads of ibises, jackals, and falcons. They are the crew, the faculties of the mind that keep the autonomic functions running while the master sleeps. They steer the rudder. They watch the banks. They are silent, terrified.

Because they can feel it coming.

The air grows heavy. It presses against your skin like a physical weight, a static pressure that makes your teeth ache. The silence of the Duat changes. It is no longer an empty silence; it is a pregnant silence. A silence that is holding its breath. The river ahead stops flowing. The boat begins to slow, dragged by an invisible friction.

Then, the smell hits you. It is not the smell of rot, for rot implies life that has passed. This is the smell of something that never lived. A metallic, ozone scent of absolute cold. The smell of the void.

Ahead, the darkness coagulates. It knots itself together. A shape rises from the oil-black river, soundless and massive. It blocks the way forward. It blocks the hope of the east. It is Apophis. The coils of the serpent are miles long, disappearing into the gloom, but the head is raised high, level with the prow of the boat.

You look up, and you wish you hadn't. The eyes of the serpent are not like the eyes of a predator. A predator looks at you with hunger, which is a form of relationship. These eyes look at you with nothing. They are swirling vortices of un-being. To look into them is to feel a sudden, seductive pull, a terrible, sweet vertigo that whispers, "Why struggle? Why carry the burden of being you? It is so hard to be separate. It is so hard to be conscious. Just let go. Come back to the dark. Come back to the sleep that has no dreams."

You feel your knees weaken. The crew stands frozen, their hands slipping from the oars. The hypnotic power of the gaze is overwhelming. The boat is drifting toward the open maw, drawn by the gravity of pure negation. Ra stirs in his sleep, a whimper of nightmares escaping his lips.

But there is one who does not freeze.

At the very front of the boat, standing alone on the prow, is a figure you had not noticed before. He is lean, wiry, his skin the color of a bruised sunset. His head is that of a strange, unidentifiable beast: long-snouted, square-eared, alert. This is Set. He is not beautiful. He is not calm. He is vibrating with a tension so tight it hums like a plucked bowstring.

He does not look at the hypnotic eyes. He knows better. He looks at the neck.

In his hands, he holds a harpoon of cold, heavy iron. His knuckles are white. He bares his teeth, and a growl rips from his throat: a sound of pure, unadulterated defiance. It is an ugly sound. It is the sound of a cornered animal refusing to die. It is the sound of life screaming "NO" to the void.

Set leaps.

He does not float; he crashes. He lands on the coils of the serpent with the weight of a collapsing mountain. He drives the iron spear down, not with grace, but with fury. A wet, tearing sound echoes through the cavern as the iron pierces the scale and sinks into the meat of the chaos-serpent.

The hypnotic spell breaks instantly. The silence shatters. Apophis roars - a sound that vibrates in your marrow - and thrashes, whipping the black river into a foaming frenzy. The boat rocks violently, threatening to capsize. But Set holds on. He is thrown left and right, battered against the scales, but his grip is iron. He twists the spear. He channels all his rage, all his chaotic power, all the storms of the desert into that single point of contact.

He pins the monster. He does not kill it (chaos cannot die) but he masters it. He forces the head down, breaking the gaze that blocked the path.

"Row!" he screams back at the frozen crew. "ROW!"

The command breaks their paralysis. The oars dip into the churning water. The boat surges past the writhing mass of the serpent, scraping against its side, moving through the danger, moving through the fear.

And as you leave the thrashing monster behind in the darkness, the pressure lifts. The air rushes back into your lungs. Set stands up, panting, wiping black ichor from his chest. He looks back at the darkness, spits once into the river, and returns to his post.

Ahead, the darkness turns grey. Then silver. Then, a pale, miraculous wash of rose-gold. The horizon. The death of the night. The sun has survived.

III. The Reflection

The myth of the Solar Barque is one of the most sophisticated maps of the psyche ever produced by the human imagination. It addresses the fundamental problem of consciousness: How does the **Ego** maintain itself against the overwhelming gravity of the **Unconscious**?

In our modern world, we tend to view consciousness (being awake, aware, and rational) as the default state. We assume we *are* conscious, and that sleep is just a break. The Egyptians, and later Carl Jung, inverted this. For them, the unconscious (darkness/sleep) is the natural, default state of the universe. Consciousness is an anomaly, a heroic effort that must be "performed" and renewed every single day (Neumann 1954).

To understand the learning of this chapter, we must break down the three key players: Ra, Apophis, and Set.

Ra represents the central operating system of our waking life: the **Ego**. This is the part of you that has a name, a job title, a social security number, and a calendar. It organizes reality. It separates "me" from "you," "yesterday" from "tomorrow." It is the principle of differentiation.

We often glorify the Ego. We want to be "lucid," "enlightened," and "rational." We strive to be like Apollo or the midday Ra: shining, perfect, and composed. This is the realm of the **Persona**, the mask of competency we wear for the world.

However, the myth shows us the secret weakness of Ra. In the depths of the unconscious (the Duat), Ra is an "old man." He is tired. Why? Because maintaining order is exhausting. Being "good," being "rational," and keeping the world organized drains the libido (psychic energy). An Ego that tries to exist *only* as pure light, repressing all darkness, becomes brittle. It lacks the vitality to defend itself (Jung 1969). This is the psychological profile of the "Nice Guy" or the "Perfect Daughter": the individual who is impeccably behaved but suffers from chronic anxiety, burnout, or a sense of hollowness. They are Ra without

Set.

If Ra is the structure of our reality (The Symbolic Order), **Apophis** is the force that seeks to dissolve that structure. In Jungian terms, Apophis is the **Negative Uroboros**, the terrible aspect of the Mother archetype. It is the desire to regress. It is the voice of depression that says, "It's too hard to be a person. Just sleep. Just give up." It represents the gravitational pull of the unconscious that threatens to swallow the ego back into a state of non-differentiation (psychosis, Neumann 1954).

In **Lacanian** terms, Apophis represents an encounter with **The Real**. The Real is that which resists symbolization. It is the traumatic void, the chaos of existence that cannot be put into words. When we face a trauma, a sudden death, or a deep depression, the "story" of our lives (the Solar Barque) stops moving. We encounter the "impossible" Real – a traumatic void that resists symbolisation (Lacan 1978).

Notice the weapon of Apophis in the retelling: **The Gaze**. He does not bite; he hypnotizes. This is the "fascination of the abyss." When we are in a state of deep neurosis or depression, we often feel paralyzed. We stare at the problem, at the pain, at the hopelessness, and we cannot look away. The more we look, the more we want to surrender to it. The "Nice Ego" (Ra) is particularly susceptible to this. It tries to reason with the depression ("I shouldn't feel this way," "I have a good life"), but you cannot reason with a snake. Logic does not work on the Real.

This brings us to the hero of the hour: **Set**. Set is the archetype of the **Shadow**. He contains all the qualities the Ego rejects: aggression, chaos, violence, unpredictability, and selfishness. In civilized society, we are taught to repress Set. We are told that anger is "bad," that aggression is "toxic," that we must be polite and agreeable.

But the myth offers a radical counter-proposal: **You cannot survive the night without your Shadow.**

When the abyss stares at you, "goodness" is not enough. You need **Aggression**. Not the aggression of a bully (which is Shadow possessing the Ego), but the aggression of a sentry (Ego possessing the Shadow). Set stands on the prow. He does not use magic words; he uses an **iron spear**. This is the "Cut" (Jung 1970).

The Lacanian Separation: In psychoanalysis, the subject needs to make a "cut" or a separation from the overwhelming desire of the Other. To avoid being swallowed by the mother's desire or the abyss of the Real, the subject must be able to say "NO." This "No" is an aggressive act.

- It is the aggression required to set a boundary with a toxic parent.
- It is the aggression required to quit a soul-sucking job.
- It is the aggression required to drag oneself out of bed during a depressive episode and force the body to move.
- It is the aggression of the artist who imposes form on chaotic matter.

In *The Ethics of Psychoanalysis* (Lacan 1992), Lacan identifies the center of the unconscious as ***Das Ding* (The Thing)**. This is the primordial, magnetic void (represented here by Apophis) that threatens to swallow the subject into a state of lethal enjoyment. To exist as a separate entity, the subject must maintain a specific distance from this void.

This is **Setian energy**: Set's role on the prow is to enforce this distance. His strike is not just violence; it is the structural **barrier** that prevents the Ego from collapsing into the abyss of the Thing. He enacts the necessary aggression required to say "No" to the seductive pull of non-existence.

The Lesson: The Solar Cycle

The profound wisdom of this myth is that the battle is **cyclical**. Ra does not kill Apophis once and for all. Apophis is immortal. He will be there again tomorrow night. Western narratives often promise "Happily Ever After", a final victory where the dragon is slain, and we live in perpetual peace. The Egyptian psyche rejects this fantasy. It asserts that mental health is not a destination; it is a **maintenance project**.

Every day, we build the ego (sunrise). Every night, we dissolve into sleep and dreams (sunset). And in the deepest darkness of our personal struggles, we must summon our inner Set to push back the encroaching chaos.

If you are feeling exhausted by the constant need to fight your demons, this myth tells you: **You are not doing it wrong.** This *is* the work. The sun does not apologize for setting, and it does not apologize for the monsters it meets in the dark. It simply employs the necessary force to rise again.

Integration Practice: Ask yourself: Where is your Set?

- Do you allow yourself to feel anger, or do you swallow it until it turns into resentment (poisoning the boat)?

- When you face a "hypnotic" problem (an addiction, a depressive thought loop), do you try to reason with it (Ra), or do you use the iron spear of decisive action (Set)?
- Are you trying to be so "good" that you have become defenseless?

To be a whole human being, you must be the Captain of the Boat (Ra), but you must also invite the Monster Hunter (Set) onto the deck. Without the monster hunter, the Captain never sees the dawn.

IV. References

- **Assmann, J.** (2001). *The Search for God in Ancient Egypt.* (D. Lorton, Trans.). Ithaca: Cornell University Press.
- **Faulkner, R. O.** (1972). *The Ancient Egyptian Book of the Dead.* London: British Museum Press.
- **Hornung, E.** (1999). *The Ancient Egyptian Books of the Afterlife.* Ithaca: Cornell University Press.
- **Jung, C. G.** (1969). *The Archetypes and the Collective Unconscious* (Collected Works of C.G. Jung, Vol. 9, Part 1). Princeton: Princeton University Press.
- **Jung, C. G.** (1970). *Mysterium Coniunctionis* (Collected Works of C.G. Jung, Vol. 14). Princeton: Princeton University Press.
- **Lacan, J.** (1992). *The Seminar of Jacques Lacan, Book VII: The Ethics of Psychoanalysis 1959–1960.* (D. Porter, Trans.). New York: W. W. Norton & Company.
- **Lacan, J.** (1978). *The Four Fundamental Concepts of Psycho-Analysis* (Book XI). New York: W. W. Norton & Company.
- **Neumann, E.** (1954). *The Origins and History of Consciousness.* Princeton: Princeton University Press.
- **Te Velde, H.** (1967). *Seth, God of Confusion: A Study of His Role in Egyptian Mythology and Religion.* Leiden: Brill.

2 THE MOON: THE REFLECTION AND THE UNCONSCIOUS

Archetype: The Mother, The Anima, Memory, Cycles
Myth: The Tale of the Bamboo Cutter (Kaguya-hime)

I. The Context: The Light That Does Not Warm

If the Sun is the burning consistency of the Ego, the Moon is something far more slippery. It is the realm of reflection. The Moon generates no light of its own. It merely mirrors the sun while transforming that light into something cool, ghostly, and hypnotic.

Psychologically, we enter the domain of the **Anima** (the inner feminine soul in the male psyche, or the relationship to the unconscious) and the **Imaginary** order. This is the world of mirrors, illusions, and the deep, watery pull of emotional memory.

Our guide for this terrain is the oldest surviving work of Japanese fiction, *Taketori Monogatari* or "The Tale of the Bamboo Cutter" (circa 10th century). While Western moon myths often focus on madness or the hunt, the Japanese psyche offers a different texture: *Mono no aware*, the pathos of things. It is a gentle, wistful sadness regarding the impermanence of beauty.

In this story, the Moon is not a place of conquest but of absolute purity and forgetfulness. It represents a state of being too perfect for the muddy, emotional reality of Earth. The tragedy here is not a war, as in the Sun chapter, but a separation. It is the story of a love that cannot be consummated because the object of that love is not essentially human.

II. The Myth

Let your attention settle on the space behind your eyes. It is a quiet space, like a garden at night. Imagine the sounds of the day fading away, replaced by the rhythmic, chirping sound of crickets in the tall grass. The air is cool on your skin. It is the kind of cool that wakes you up and makes you feel more alive, more present in your own body.

As you walk through this imaginary garden, you find yourself in a grove of bamboo. The stalks are tall, towering high above you, swaying gently in a wind you cannot feel. They knock against each other with a hollow, wooden sound. Click. Clack. A rhythm of nature that has no urgency.

Deep in this grove, there is a man. He is an old cutter, his hands rough and stained with the green of the stalk. He is working, just as he has worked every day for fifty years. But today is different. Today, in the deepest shadow of the grove, he sees a light.

It is not the warm, yellow light of the sun. It is a pale, blue-white luminescence, glowing from the base of a single bamboo stalk. It pulses gently, like a heartbeat. The old man, overcome by a curiosity that feels like a spell, raises his axe. With one clean stroke, he severs the stalk.

Inside, nestled in the hollow joint of the bamboo, is a child. She is tiny, no bigger than his thumb, glowing with that same ethereal light. She is perfect. She is quiet. She is the answer to a prayer he never spoke aloud.

He takes her home to his wife. They place her in a tiny basket, but the magic of the moon is swift and relentless. In mere months, the child transforms. She does not grow like a human child; she unfolds like a blossom in fast-motion. She becomes a woman of breathtaking, impossible beauty. They name her Kaguya-hime, The Shining Princess of the Supple Bamboo. And with her arrival, the earth itself seems to change. Every stalk the old man cuts now contains a nugget of gold. The poverty of the bamboo cutter vanishes, replaced by a wealth that feels heavy, unearned, and strange.

But it is her beauty that disturbs the world. It is not earthly. It does not invite touch. It creates a distance. When you look at her, you feel a longing that aches in your chest, a desire for something you cannot name and cannot have.

News of this impossible creature travels on the wind, reaching the capital. Men come. Commoners, merchants, samurai. They line the fence of the bamboo cutter's house, hoping for a glimpse of her robe, a shadow on the screen. Most lose heart and leave. But five men remain. These are the Suitors of High Rank, three Princes and two Grand Counselors. These are men who believe that the world is a catalogue of things to be owned, and that Kaguya-hime is simply the most expensive item in the catalogue.

They camp outside her fence for months. They endure the freezing rain of winter and the stifling heat of summer. They send letters written on paper dusted with gold, poems filled with the desperate, inflated language of the ego that refuses to hear "no."

Finally, the old bamboo cutter, moved by their persistence and fearing their rank, begs his daughter to choose. Kaguya-hime sits behind her screen, her voice cool as a mountain stream. "I will not marry a man for his rank," she says. "I will marry the one who can prove the depth of his devotion. I will set a task for each."

To Prince Ishizukuri, she says: "Bring me the Stone Begging Bowl used by the Lord Buddha in India." To Prince Kuramochi, she says: "Bring me a Branch made of Gold and Silver, with Pearls for fruit, from the floating mountain of Penglai." To the Minister of the Right, Abe no Miushi: "Bring me the Robe of the Fire-Rat, which does not burn." To the Grand Counselor Otomo: "Bring me the Jewel that glows in many colors from the neck of the Dragon." To the Middle Counselor Isonokami: "Bring me the Cowry Shell born from a Swallow."

She asks for things that do not exist in the known world. She asks for the impossible.

The princes scatter, driven by the madness of their own desire. They do not understand that the tasks are symbolic; they treat them as logistical problems. And so begins the comedy of errors, the frantic thrashing of the ego against the impossible.

Prince Ishizukuri is lazy. He does not go to India. He goes to a nearby temple in Kyoto, takes a dirty, blackened bowl from an altar, wraps it in silk, and presents it to the princess. Kaguya-hime unwraps it. She does not need magic to see the truth. She sees the dust of Kyoto, not the dust of India. She sees the lack of light. She writes a poem mocking his "bowl of shame" and sends him away.

Prince Kuramochi is cleverer. He tells everyone he is sailing to the floating islands. In reality, he hides in a secret cellar with six master jewelers. For three years, they work day and night, forging a branch of pure gold with pearls for berries. It is a masterpiece of artifice. When he presents it, the old bamboo cutter is fooled. He thinks it is a miracle. But just as the Prince is boasting of his dangerous journey, the six jewelers burst into the courtyard, demanding their wages. The illusion shatters. The Prince covers his face and flees into the night, his honor dissolved.

Minister Abe buys a robe from a merchant who claims it is the skin of the Fire-Rat. It is a magnificent blue fur. He presents it with great pomp. Kaguya-hime says, "If it is truly the Fire-Rat's skin, it will not burn. Put it in the fire." The Minister, confident in his purchase, throws it into the coals. In an instant, it bursts into green flames and turns to ash. He stands staring at the soot, realizing he bought a lie.

The Grand Counselor Otomo takes the quest seriously. He sails into the stormy seas to find a dragon. But the ocean rises against him. A storm batters his ship for days. He falls sick with terror, his eyes glued shut with salt, praying to the gods to save him, renouncing his desire for the princess if only the sea will let him live. He washes ashore, broken, half-dead, and swollen. He learns that the Dragon, the unconscious, is not something you can rob.

And the Middle Counselor, seeking the swallow's shell, climbs high onto a roof to peer into a nest. He loses his footing and falls, breaking his back. He dies not from a dragon, but from a slip of the foot, grasping at a bird's nest.

They are broken against the rock of the impossible. Kaguya-hime watches their failure with a calm, detached sadness. She does not enjoy their suffering, but she cannot accept their humanity. Their desire is heavy, sticky, and earthly. It seeks to possess. She belongs to a different order.

Then, the Emperor comes.

He does not come to buy her. He does not send servants. He hears of her beauty and organizes a hunt near the bamboo cutter's lands, hoping to catch a glimpse of this light that has humbled his greatest ministers. When he enters the house, Kaguya-hime tries to hide, fading into a shimmering light. But the Emperor sees her. He catches her by the sleeve.

For a moment, he is struck dumb. He sees a face that shines with the brilliance of a thousand full moons. He offers to take her to the palace. "I cannot go," she says. "I am not born of your country. If you force me, I will vanish like mist."

The Emperor, unlike the princes, listens. He releases her sleeve. He realizes that to hold her is to lose her. He returns to his palace, leaving her behind, but he leaves his heart in the bamboo grove.

Thus begins a courtship of the spirit. He writes her poems. He enters the realm of symbols. He speaks to her of the loneliness of the throne, of the changing seasons, of the light of the moon on the palace roof. A correspondence begins, a delicate thread of ink and paper connecting the highest power of the Earth with the daughter of the Sky.

For three years, they exchange letters. The Emperor offers her his vulnerability, not his possessions. And for the first time, Kaguya-hime feels a ripple in the stillness of her own being. She writes back. "If I were born to this world, I would not hide myself from you." It is an admission of possibility, a confession that if she were human, he would be the one. She begins to understand love, not as possession, but as resonance.

But the seasons turn. The air grows crisp. The crickets in the garden change their song to a slower, mournful rhythm. The full moon of the eighth month approaches, hanging lower and larger in the sky than ever before. And a change comes over the princess.

She begins to weep. It is not the weeping of sadness, but the weeping of resonance. She sits on the veranda, looking up at the great white orb, and her body begins to tremble.

And with every glance upward, you might notice a resonance beginning to build... a vibration that starts not in the air, but deep inside the marrow. It is as if an invisible tuning fork has been struck in the high heavens, and her bones, perhaps even your own, begin to hum in sympathy. She feels a tug in the blood... a slow, heavy tidal pull that speaks to the salt water within. It is a gravity reversed, a pull so inviting, so overwhelming, that her hands instinctively find the rough, cold wood of the veranda pillars... gripping the grain, grounding the body, just to keep from surrendering to that weightless desire to simply... let go... and float away. It is the call of the origin. It is the cellular memory of a home that is cold, perfect, and silent.

She realizes with a terrifying clarity. "I am not from here. And they are calling me back."

She tells the old parents. They weep. She tells the Emperor in a letter. He sends an army. On the night of the full moon, two thousand imperial guards surround the house. They stand on the roof. They stand in the garden. Their bows are drawn, arrow tips pointed at the zenith. They are men of war, ready to kill anything that moves. They believe that steel can stop the divine.

It begins as a silence. The crickets stop. The wind dies. The world holds its breath.

Then, the light descends.

It is not a beam; it is a weight. A radiant, crushing presence that presses down on the house. It is ten times brighter than the full moon, yet it casts no shadows. It is a light that dissolves perspective. It is a light that has no warmth.

The guards look up, and their will simply evaporates. Their arms, holding the bows, become heavy as lead. It is not that they are afraid. It is that they are rendered insignificant. It is a physiological impossibility to fight. The synapses that command violence simply stop firing. In the face of this absolute, cold perfection, the desire to assert the ego feels absurd. Weapons drop from numb fingers, clattering onto the roof tiles. Strong men fall to their knees, paralyzed by a beauty that is utterly indifferent to them.

A cloud descends, carrying the Lunar Host. They are beings of exquisite geometry, their robes flowing without the disturbance of wind. They float a few feet above the ground, untouched by the dust. They do not look at the guards. They do not look at the parents. They look only at the one who belongs to them.

The doors of the inner chamber fly open. Kaguya-hime walks out. She cannot help herself. Her body is answering the call. The old bamboo cutter throws himself at her feet, weeping, begging. Kaguya-hime looks down, and tears fill her eyes one last time. She touches his face. The connection is still there. The human heart is still beating, fighting the celestial tide.

The leader of the Moon People approaches. He holds a robe of feathers. It shimmers with a color that has no name. "Come," he says. "You have been in this unclean place long enough."

Kaguya-hime hesitates. She writes one last letter to the Emperor, pouring her remaining humanity into the ink. She places a small jar of the Elixir of Life beside it. Then, she stands straight.

The Robe of Forgetfulness is placed upon her shoulders.

The change is instantaneous. The tension leaves her shoulders. The tears stop mid-fall. The light in her eyes shifts from the warm, moist depth of human emotion to the cool, flat reflection of a mirror. She looks at the old man, and there is no recognition. No love. No hate. Only a pristine, terrible clarity. The memories of the earth, the smell of the bamboo, the pain of the princes, the poetry of the Emperor, are wiped clean.

She steps into the palanquin. The cloud rises. The light withdraws, sucking the magic out of the air, leaving the garden dark, the guards weeping in the dirt, and the old man grasping at empty air.

III. The Reflection

The story of Kaguya-hime is a heartbreaking meditation on the nature of the **Anima** and the structural necessity of loss in the formation of the self.

The Unattainable Anima and the Impossible Tasks

In Jungian psychology, the Anima is the archetype of **Zoé**, infinite, indestructible life. Unlike *Bios* (the biographical life of the ego which has a beginning and an end), *Zoé* is the raw, impersonal current of vitality that flows through us. She is the chaotic, animating force connecting the rational ego to the deep unconscious.

Kaguya-hime represents a specific aspect of this archetype: the **Celestial Anima** or the "Soul-Image" that refuses to be grounded. She is the "Moon Princess" who cannot be married.

The suitors represent the Ego's immature attempts to possess this soul-image. Notice how they approach her. They try to transact. They believe that if they perform a feat or buy an object, they are "owed" the soul.

The Stone Bowl is the attempt to fake spiritual depth. The Prince takes a dirty object and calls it holy. The Jeweled Branch represents the attempt to use artifice and craft, hiring jewelers to mimic organic growth. The Fire-Rat Robe is the reliance on commerce and the exotic, while the Dragon Jewel shows the hubris of trying to steal from the unconscious by force.

Kaguya-hime rejects them not out of cruelty, but out of necessity. The Soul cannot be bought, tricked, or stolen. The tasks are "impossible" because the Ego cannot integrate the Anima through force or materialism. If the Ego were to fully possess the unconscious, if the Moon were to crash into the Earth, the result would be catastrophe or psychosis (Jung 1968). The Anima must remain somewhat "other" to function as a guide. She acts as a lure, pulling the Ego toward growth via the impossible tasks, teaching us that the feminine principle cannot be possessed by will, but only related to through endurance (Von Franz 1972).

The Mirror Stage and the Robe of Forgetfulness

From a Lacanian perspective, the Moon is the ultimate mirror. In the famous **Mirror Stage**, the infant sees its reflection and misrecognizes it as a whole, perfect self. This "Ideal-I" is mesmerizing. It is glowing, complete, and beautiful (Lacan 2006).

Kaguya-hime acts as this mirror for the characters in the story. The old bamboo cutter sees in her the perfect daughter. The princes see the perfect wife. The Emperor sees the perfect empress. They project their deepest desires onto her blank, glowing surface. She functions as the **Objet petit a** (the object cause of desire). She causes desire specifically *because* she is lacking. She is the glowing impossibility that is always just out of reach.

The tragedy of the story lies in the **Robe of Forgetfulness**. On Earth, we suffer. We feel the pain of separation, aging, and loss. This suffering is the "impurity" the moon people despise. But Lacan would argue that this suffering is exactly what makes us subjects. To be a human subject is to be "castrated" to accept loss and limitation.

When Kaguya-hime puts on the Robe, she returns to the Imaginary Order. She returns to a state of absolute wholeness where there is no pain, no lack, and no memory. But the price of this wholeness is her humanity. She ceases to be a subject. She becomes an object again, a cold, distant light.

The Elixir on the Mountain

The story ends with a profound act of renunciation. Kaguya-hime leaves behind the **Elixir of Life** (immortality) for the Emperor. This is the ultimate test. The Ego is offered the chance to become like the Moon: immortal, unchanging, and perfect.

What is not written in our recounting of the tale is that the Emperor refuses. In a moment of supreme wisdom, he asks what the use of living forever is if he cannot be with her.

He takes the elixir to the highest peak in Japan, Mount Fuji, and burns it.

This is the psychological resolution. The Emperor refuses the fantasy of wholeness. He chooses to accept his mortality and his loss. In burning the elixir, the smoke rises to the moon, creating a bridge of "memory" between the earth and the sky.

This teaches us a difficult lesson about our own inner lives. We often chase the "Moon Princess" in the form of the perfect job, the perfect partner, or the perfect state of enlightenment. We believe that once we catch it, we will be complete. We will be immortal. The myth tells us we cannot keep the Moon. We can only experience its light for a season. The goal of psychological maturity is not to capture the princess and lock her in a room, but to let her go, and to find meaning in the smoke that rises from the loss (Keene 1967).

The smoke is our art. The smoke is our poetry. The smoke is the book you are writing. It is the residue of our attempt to touch the divine, proving that while we cannot live on the moon, we have not forgotten it.

Integration Practice: Burning the Elixir

Ask yourself: Where is Kaguya-hime living in your psyche right now?

- Identify an area where you are demanding perfection or absolute purity. Is it a relationship you want to be flawless? A career you expect to fulfill your every need? This is your "Moon."
- Notice if you are trying to "buy" this ideal like the Princes (through effort/money) or command it like the Emperor (through willpower).
- Consider the pain of the gap between that ideal and your reality. Do you try to numb that pain (The Robe of Forgetfulness)? Or are you willing to "burn the elixir", to accept the loss and transmute it into something creative?

Practice: When you feel the ache of unfulfilled desire, instead of rushing to fix it, let it sit. Imagine that ache as the smoke rising from Mount Fuji. It is not a sign of failure; it is the evidence of your humanity connecting with the divine.

IV. References

- **Jung, C. G.** (1968). *Psychology and Alchemy* (Collected Works of C.G. Jung, Vol. 12). Princeton: Princeton University Press.
- **Keene, D.** (1967). *Japanese Literature: An Introduction for Western Readers.* New York: Grove Press.

- **Lacan, J.** (2006). *Écrits: The First Complete Edition in English.* (B. Fink, Trans.). New York: W. W. Norton & Company.

- **Richardson, M.** (2016). *The Tale of the Bamboo Cutter.* [Translation and Commentary]. CreateSpace Independent Publishing Platform.

- **Von Franz, M. L.** (1972). *Problems of the Feminine in Fairytales.* Dallas: Spring Publications.

3 MERCURY: THE TRICKSTER AND THE WORD

Archetype: The Messenger, The Trickster, Intellect, Liminality
Myth: The Cycle of Tokjuaj (Wichí/Argentina)

I. The Context: The God of the Crossroads

In the classical ordering of the cosmos, Mercury (Hermes) is the swiftest of the gods. He is the messenger, the ruler of communication, commerce, and thieves. He is the only Olympian allowed to travel freely between the heights of Olympus, the world of men, and the depths of Hades. He is the god of the boundary, the *limen.*

Psychologically, Mercury represents the **Intellect** and the function of the **Trickster**. He is the fluid, adaptable energy of the mind that creates connections between disparate things. He is the inventor of language, but also the inventor of the lie. He teaches us that truth is not a static rock, but a moving target.

To explore this archetype, we leave the marble halls of Greece and travel to the dry, thorny forests of the Gran Chaco in South America, specifically to the mythology of the Wichí people of northern Argentina (Métraux 1946; Terán 1994). Here, the Mercurial energy is not a boy with winged sandals. He is **Tokjuaj**, often called "The Uncle."

Tokjuaj is a Demiurge. He created the world, but not through divine plan or benevolent wisdom. He created it through trial and error, through accident, and often through pure, unadulterated mischief (Wilbert & Simoneau 1982). He is the ultimate figure of the Unconscious Intellect. He is brilliant, destructive, hilarious, and terrifyingly creative. He shows us that the mind is not a disciplined soldier. The mind is a wild animal that shapes reality through its hunger and its play.

II. The Myth

Let your attention turn inward, or perhaps just let your gaze soften until the edges of the room blur into a haze. I want you to imagine heat. Not the pleasant warmth of a summer beach, but a heavy, pressing heat. The kind of heat that smells of dry dust and resin. You are in the Gran Chaco. The forest here is made of thorns. The trees are twisted, hard as iron, protecting their water from the sun. The earth is pale and cracked.

It is silent here. The cicadas are vibrating with a sound that is less like a noise and more like a headache made audible. And walking through this landscape, kicking up small clouds of dust with his calloused feet, is a man. Or at least, he looks like a man.

This is Tokjuaj. He is old, yet his movements are spry, jerky, and filled with a restless energy. His eyes are black and darting. He is looking for something. He is always looking for something. Usually, he is looking for trouble.

He is hungry. His hunger is not just a physical need. It is a cosmic force. It is the hunger of the void wanting to be filled. He walks until he comes to a great expanse of dry earth where the river used to be. The fish are trapped in muddy pools, gasping for air. A "good" creator might save them. Tokjuaj does not save them. He eats them. He eats until his belly is distended, until he can barely move.

But Tokjuaj is bored. A full belly creates a still mind, and Tokjuaj hates stillness. He needs movement. He needs a story.

He sees a Jaguar. The Jaguar is the Lord of the Forest, sleek, powerful, and terrifying. Tokjuaj looks at his own hands, which are weak. He looks at his own teeth, which are flat. He feels a sudden, sharp spike of envy. He wants that power. But he knows he cannot fight the Jaguar. Mercury cannot fight Mars. He must use the only weapon he has. The Word.

Tokjuaj approaches the Jaguar, feigning a limp. He makes his face a mask of concern. "Nephew," he says. In Wichí myth, he is everyone's uncle. "Nephew, a great storm is coming. The wind will be so strong it will strip the skin from your bones. Look at the sky."

The Jaguar looks up. The sky is blue. Empty. But Tokjuaj points with such conviction, his voice trembling with such specific, detailed terror, that the Jaguar begins to doubt his own eyes. The Trickster attacks reality itself. He paints a picture with words that overlays the world.

"I am old," Tokjuaj says. "I have seen this before. I will tie myself to this algarrobo tree so I am not blown away. You should do the same, Nephew. You are strong, but the wind cares nothing for strength."

The Jaguar, infected by the anxiety of the intellect, agrees. He allows Tokjuaj to bind him to the tree with strong leather vines. Tokjuaj ties the knots tight. He pulls them until the Jaguar winces. "Is it tight enough, Nephew?" he asks. "Can you move?"

"I cannot move," the Jaguar growls.

Tokjuaj steps back. The mask of concern vanishes. His face splits into a grin that is all teeth and malice. He picks up a heavy stone. "Now," he says, "let us see who is the Lord of the Forest."

He does not kill the Jaguar. That would be too final, and Tokjuaj has no use for endings. He prefers the game. Instead, he torments him. He dances around the bound predator, poking the tender nose with a stick, whispering insults that sting worse than the thorns. He takes a handful of charcoal and ash, rubbing it into the Jaguar's golden coat, smudging the perfect rosettes, metaphorically stealing the spots that signify his power. He scoops up the fine, choking dust of the riverbed and throws it into the Jaguar's wide, furious eyes, blinding the king with the very earth he thought he ruled. And then, he laughs. It is not a warm laugh. It is the dry, rattling laughter of the mind triumphing over matter. It is the cruel, electric joy of the intellect realizing that with a few words and a piece of leather, it can turn the brute force of the world into a whimpering toy.

But the cycle of Tokjuaj turns. The Trickster who tricks is always tricked in return. This is the law of the liminal; the return of the shadow.

Tokjuaj walks on, wearing the Jaguar's spots, feeling invincible. He comes to a village. But this is not a village of men. It is a village of women. They are beautiful, working the chaguar fibers, laughing. Tokjuaj feels a new hunger. It is not for food this time. It is Eros. It is the drive to merge.

He struts into the village, confident in his stolen power. He chooses the most beautiful woman. He woos her not with truth, but with the slippery, glittering currency of the imagination. He weaves stories of travels he never took, painting landscapes of impossible abundance where the rivers run with honey and the trees bow down with fruit just for her. He speaks of food, roasted armadillo dripping with fat, honeycombs bursting with sweetness, until the air in the village seems to smell of a feast that isn't there. His voice is a low hum, vibrating in her chest, bypassing logic, speaking directly to hunger. She smiles, her eyes glazing over, caught in the web of a reality that exists only because he says it does. She invites him into her hut.

But Tokjuaj does not know the secret of this ancient time. In the beginning, women were not as they are now. They were dangerous. They possessed toothed vaginas. They were the devourers. The entry to the womb was guarded by rows of sharp, obsidian teeth.

Tokjuaj pushes aside the leather flap and enters the hut. The darkness inside is absolute. It is a physical weight, pressing against his eyes, smelling of earth, dried herbs, and a musk that makes his pulse hammer in his throat. He does not think. He does not plan. He is pulled forward by a gravity older than his own mind. He reaches out into the blackness, his hands trembling not with fear, but with the electric, blind compulsion of the body seeking its other half.

And then, a scream rips through the silence of the Chaco. It is a scream of pain, of shock, of sudden, brutal castration. Tokjuaj flees the hut, bleeding, humbled, his manhood damaged.

He runs back into the forest, howling. The Jaguar's spots fall off. He is just a man again. An old, foolish man.

But Tokjuaj does not die. He cannot die. He is not defeated.

He sits by the riverbank, the water cooling his wounds, but the fire in his mind is just beginning to catch. He is done feeling. Now, he is thinking. He scans the riverbed, his eyes narrowing, filtering out the beautiful stones, looking only for the useful ones. He finds a piece of flint, grey and unforgiving. He strikes it against a boulder with a sharp crack, flaking away the softness, revealing the cutting edge hidden inside. He tests the weight in his palm. It is balanced. It is cold. It is an instrument of will.

He returns to the village when the moon is hidden behind the clouds. The silence is heavy. He moves through the sleeping camp, not with the swagger of a seducer, but with the silent, terrifying purpose of a surgeon entering an operating theater. He pushes aside the leather flap. The air inside is thick with the smell of sleep.

He approaches the sleeping woman. This time, there is no lust in his hands, only a clinical, detached precision. He separates the flesh. He sees the glint of the teeth in the dark, the rows of serrated obsidian that guard the mystery. He raises his stone chisel. He strikes.

It is a delicate violence. Chip by chip, he breaks the teeth of the mother-destroyer. He works with a rhythm: strike, pause, grind. He smoothes the jagged shards into harmless curves. He reshapes the biology of terror into the biology of pleasure and life. He works down the line, from hut to hut, an architect of the body, modifying the raw, dangerous Real until it fits the specifications of the future.

He created sexual reproduction. He created the future of the human race. Not because he was noble. Not because he wanted to save humanity. But because he was horny and he solved a problem.

This is the way of Tokjuaj. He stumbles. He breaks things. He gets hurt. And in the process of fixing his own messes, he invents the world. He creates the river to cool his burns. He creates the color of the birds to hide from his enemies. He teaches men to weave nets so they don't have to be as hungry as he was.

He is the accident that becomes the law.

As he walks away from the village, healing, changing shape once more into a caracara hawk to fly on the thermals, you can feel the air around him shifting. It is electric. It is unstable. He is the force that keeps the world from becoming stiff. He is the reminder that everything you think is solid, your identity, your safety, your moral code, is just a story he hasn't decided to rewrite yet.

III. The Reflection

The figure of Tokjuaj offers us a raw, undiluted look at the **Trickster** archetype, which is the shadow side of the messenger Mercury. In our sanitized Western view, we often mistake the Intellect for a tool of order, something used to build bridges, write laws, and organize spreadsheets. Tokjuaj reminds us that the Intellect is fundamentally chaotic.

The Shadow of the Creator

In Jungian analysis, the Trickster is the "Shadow of the Self." If the Self is the image of wholeness and order, represented by the Mandala, the Trickster is the image of fragmentation and fluidity. Tokjuaj is a creator god, but he creates through **bricolage** or tinkering (Lévi-Strauss 1962). He does not have a plan. He has a drive.

This is a profound psychological insight into human creativity. We often believe that we need a "perfect plan" before we start a project or a new phase of life. We want to be like the biblical God, speaking light into existence with perfect authority. But the human psyche works like Tokjuaj. We stumble. We make mistakes. We get wounded or castrated by our encounters with reality. It is in the repair of those wounds that we create something new. The artist creates because they are trying to solve an inner conflict. The scientist discovers the cure by accident while looking for something else. The personality is forged not in the successes, but in the embarrassing failures that force us to adapt.

Jung argues that the Trickster is the archetype of the **pre-conscious** stage of development. He represents the mind before it has developed a Superego or morality. He is driven by the Id. Yet, without this amoral, hungry energy, there is no change. A psyche without a Trickster is stagnant. It is a Jaguar tied to a tree: strong, but immobile (Jung 1959).

The Sliding Signifier

From a post-Lacanian perspective, specifically that of **Slavoj Žižek**, Tokjuaj represents the volatile nature of the **Signifier** before it is anchored by the "Quilting Point" (*Point de capiton*). Žižek elaborates that meaning is not inherent in words; rather, words are a sliding chain that only momentarily pauses when a "Master Signifier" (like God, The Nation, or The Law) pins them down, retroactively creating meaning (Žižek 1989).

Tokjuaj is the active un-doing of this Quilting Point. When he speaks to the Jaguar, he uses language to create a reality that does not exist, such as the storm.

He pulls out the "pin" of Truth, allowing the signifiers to slide again. This reveals the terrifying freedom of the Symbolic Order: we can use words to construct entirely new, deceptive worlds.

Consider the incident with the "toothed women." In this framework, this is the encounter with the **Real**, the traumatic kernel that resists symbolization. The teeth represent the raw, terrifying excess of enjoyment (*Jouissance*) that threatens to swallow the subject. Tokjuaj's intervention, breaking the teeth, is the act of instituting the Symbolic Order. He uses a tool (Techné) to "castrate" the Real, modifying it so that it can be integrated into the social link of marriage and reproduction. He transforms a deadly trauma into a livable structure.

This is the ultimate function of Mercury. He mediates between the deadly, raw drives of the body (the Real) and the structured world of society. He is the diplomat who negotiates with the monsters in the dark. He does not kill them like a hero. He operates on them. He changes their nature.

The Necessity of Mischief

Why do we need Tokjuaj? Why can't we just have Apollo? Because order eventually becomes tyranny. When our lives become too rigid, when we are too obsessed with being "right," "good," or "productive," we become brittle. We lose our vitality.

Tokjuaj enters the system to break the rules. He brings the accident that forces a reboot. He is the slip of the tongue that reveals the truth we were hiding. He is the sudden loss of a job that forces us to find our true vocation. To integrate Mercury is to develop a sense of **Humor** about one's own existence. It is the ability to look at your own disasters, your own foolishness, and laugh the laugh of Tokjuaj. It is realizing that you are not the Jaguar, the serious, powerful ego. You are the one who ties the knots, and sometimes, the one who gets bit.

Integration Practice: The Sacred Glitch

Ask yourself: Where is your life too rigid?

- Identify an area where you are taking yourself with deadly seriousness. Is it your spiritual practice? Your diet? Your professional image? This is the Jaguar tied to the tree.

- Invite Tokjuaj. Allow yourself to do something "wrong" or "silly" in that domain. Break a small rule. Tell a joke at a funeral (metaphorically). Introduce a glitch.

- Observe the chaos not with fear, but with curiosity. What new thing is trying to be born from the mess?

Practice: The next time a plan fails or an accident happens, instead of spiraling into anger, pause. Imagine Tokjuaj sitting next to you, grinning. Ask him: "What are you trying to build from this wreckage?"

IV. References

- **Jung, C. G.** (1959). *The Archetypes and the Collective Unconscious* (Collected Works of C.G. Jung, Vol. 9, Part 1). Princeton: Princeton University Press.

- **Lévi-Strauss, C.** (1966). *The Savage Mind.* New York: Harper & Row.

- **Métraux, A.** (1946). *Myths of the Toba and Pilagá Indians of the Gran Chaco.* Philadelphia: American Folklore Society.

- **Terán, B.** (1994). *Lo que cuentan los wichís*. Buenos Aires: Ediciones del Sol.

- **Wilbert, J., & Simoneau, K.** (1982). *Folk Literature of the Mataco Indians.* Los Angeles: UCLA Latin American Center Publications.

- **Žižek, S.** (1989). *The Sublime Object of Ideology.* London: Verso.

4 VENUS: EROS AND THE OBJECT OF DESIRE

Archetype: The Lover, Value, Aesthetics, Union, Harmony
Myth: Psyche and Eros (Roman/Greek)

I. The Context: The Architecture of Longing

In the astrological pantheon, Venus is often reduced to the goddess of romance and aesthetic pleasure. She is seen as the benefactor of artists and lovers, the planet of sugar and silk. But this view is superficial. In the deeper currents of the psyche, Venus represents the principle of **Connection**. She is the force that binds the separate atoms of the universe into molecules, and separate souls into relationships.

She is gravity applied to the spirit.

However, connection is not a peaceful process. To connect with another is to lose the integrity of the self. It is a violation of the ego's borders. It is to become vulnerable, essentially enacting Lacan's famous dictum: *aimer, c'est donner ce qu'on n'a pas* ("to love is to give what one does not have") (Lacan 2015).

As such, the myths of Venus are rarely simple stories of happiness. They are stories of trial, loss, and the terrifying vulnerability required to let another person in.

To understand this archetype, we turn to the most complete and psychologically rich myth in the Western canon: the story of **Psyche and Eros** (Cupid), recorded by the Roman writer Apuleius in his novel *The Golden Ass* (2nd Century AD). It is not just a love story. It is the story of how the human soul (Psyche) earns the right to love the divine (Eros). It teaches us that love is not a feeling we fall into. It is a labor we perform.

II. The Myth

Allow your body to settle into a position of absolute ease. You might notice the weight of your hands resting in your lap, or the gentle pressure of the chair against your back. As you focus on that pressure, you can begin to imagine it not as a chair, but as the warm, supportive stone of an ancient temple. The air around you is smelling of crushed roses and sea salt. You are standing on a cliff edge, looking out over a Mediterranean sea that is so blue it looks like ink.

There is a girl standing next to you. Her name is Psyche. She is mortal, yet she is so beautiful that the locals have stopped worshipping at the altars of Venus. They worship her instead. This is a dangerous beauty. It is a beauty that isolates. No man dares to marry her. They only look. She is a statue of flesh, worshipped but untouched, lonely in the midst of a crowd.

Venus, the Great Mother, looks down from Olympus. Her jealousy is cold and sharp. She calls her son, Eros, the god of love. He is not a chubby cherub. He is a young man of terrifying power, armed with gold-tipped arrows that can unmake the mind of a philosopher or a king. "Go," she whispers. "Make her fall in love with the vilest, most broken monster on earth. Punish her for her beauty."

Eros flies down. He lands in her bedroom while she sleeps. He pulls an arrow. But as he leans over her, the candlelight catches her face. His hand trembles. For the first time in the history of the universe, Love falls in love. He pricks his own finger on the arrow. The hunter becomes the prey.

Psyche's destiny shifts. The Oracle of Apollo commands her father to leave her on a high mountain crag to be wed to a "winged serpent" that terrorizes the gods. She is dressed in funeral robes. She is abandoned on the rock, waiting for death. The wind howls around her. She closes her eyes, expecting the bite of the monster.

But death does not come. Instead, she feels a softness. The West Wind, Zephyrus, lifts her gently from the stone. It is a sensation of weightlessness, a surrender to a force that is strong but kind. It carries her down from the jagged peaks, down into a hidden valley where the air is sweet and still, depositing her on a bed of soft grass.

She wakes in a palace that has no walls, or perhaps walls made of light. It is a place of impossible luxury. Invisible servants bring her nectar and ambrosia, their voices whispering like the rustle of leaves. "We are here to serve you," they say. "You are the mistress of this house."

And when the night falls, dense and velvety, her husband comes to her.

He is invisible. The darkness is absolute. She cannot see his face. She can only feel him. And what she feels is not a monster. It is a skin softer than silk, a voice that sounds like the hum of bees in summer, a touch that bypasses her fear and speaks directly to her blood. He loves her with a divine intensity. He makes her body sing in ways she did not know were possible.

He is the lover every soul dreams of: present, passionate, and overwhelmingly real.

But he gives her one condition. A single prohibition that hangs in the dark air. "You must never see my face. If you look at me with your eyes, I will be gone forever. Love me in the dark, Psyche. Trust the feeling, not the image."

For a time, this is paradise. She lives in the bliss of the blind. She is loved. She is full. She learns to navigate by touch, by scent, by the rhythm of his breathing.

But the human mind hates a mystery. It cannot bear the unknown. Her sisters come to the edge of the valley, wailing for her supposed death. Psyche, in her naivety, invites them in. They see the palace. They see the jewels. And their grief turns instantly to green, corrosive envy.

They sit with her, holding her hands, whispering poison. "You say he is kind," the eldest says, her voice low and sharp. "But why does he hide? A man who hides his face has something to hide. The Oracle said he was a serpent. Perhaps he is shedding his skin at night. Perhaps he is fattening you up. He is not loving you, Psyche. He is tasting you."

The doubt is a seed. It falls into the fertile soil of Psyche's fear. It grows in the dark. It wraps its vines around her trust, choking it. Night after night, as she lies in the arms of the god, she feels a shiver of terror. Is this skin, or is it a scale? Is this a kiss, or a bite?

One night, while Eros sleeps beside her, heavy and warm, Psyche breaks the vow. She rises from the bed. Her hands are trembling. She lights a small oil lamp. She takes a sharp knife, prepared to sever the head of the serpent.

She creeps to the bedside. The shadows dance on the walls. She raises the lamp high.

The light falls on the bed. There is no monster. There is no serpent. There is the most beautiful being in creation. Golden curls frame a face of heartbreaking perfection. Wings that shimmer like pearl spring from his shoulders, soft and downy. He is not a beast; he is the source of all beauty. The knife falls from her hand with a clatter. She falls to her knees, trembling with a mixture of shame and awe, drinking in the sight of him, trying to memorize the curve of his mouth, the arch of his brow.

But her hand shakes. She leans too close. A single drop of scalding hot oil falls from the lamp.

It lands on the god's shoulder. The white skin blisters.

Eros wakes with a cry of pain. He sees the light. He sees the knife. He sees the betrayal. He does not rage. He does not strike her. He looks at her with a sorrow that is deeper than the ocean, a sorrow that breaks the world. He spreads his great wings.

"Love cannot live where there is no trust," he says.

And then, with a sound like a rushing wind, he is gone. The palace vanishes. The garden vanishes. The soft grass turns to cold, hard rock. Psyche is left alone in the wilderness, holding nothing but a burnt-out lamp and the echo of his voice.

She wanders the world, searching. She throws herself into rivers, but the rivers wash her ashore, refusing to take her life. She walks until her feet bleed, asking the birds, the trees, the stones if they have seen him. Finally, desperate, realizing that no earthly power can help her, she goes to the source. She goes to the mother. She surrenders herself to Venus.

Venus laughs. It is a cruel, triumphant sound that rattles the teeth. She looks at the girl who dared to be beautiful. "You want him back?" she asks. "You, a simple mortal, want to reclaim a god? Then you must prove you are worthy. You must do the work."

She sets four tasks. Four impossibilities.

First, Venus takes her to a massive granary room. In the center is a chaotic, mountain-sized pile of seeds: wheat, barley, millet, poppy, lentils, and beans, all mixed together in a hopeless tangle. "Sort them," Venus commands. "Separate every single grain by kind. Have it done by evening, or you die."

Psyche looks at the mountain of grain. It would take a hundred lifetimes. Her rational mind breaks. She sits in the dirt and weeps, waiting for the end. But nature is listening. An ant, a tiny speck of black determination, appears near her foot. Then another. Then a million. The colony arrives, a moving river of insect intelligence. They do not think; they act. With mechanical precision, they carry the grains one by one. Wheat to the left. Barley to the right. The chaos is organized by the collective instinct. When Venus returns at sunset, the work is done.

Second, Venus points to a riverbank where golden rams are grazing. Their fleece is pure gold, thick and heavy. But they are not gentle sheep. They are aggressive, charged with the solar fury of the sun. They butt heads with the force of thunder. "Bring me their wool," Venus commands.

Psyche moves toward the river, ready to throw herself among the beasts, knowing she will be trampled. But a green reed, bending in the water, whispers to her. "Do not approach them now, little one. They are filled with the heat of the day. They are dangerous with power. Wait. Wait until the sun sets. Wait until the shadows lengthen and the heat leaves their blood. When they sleep, simply gather the wool that clings to the briars." Psyche waits. She learns the art of timing. She gathers the gold without the violence.

Third, Venus demands a crystal flask filled with water from the River Styx, the source of the underworld. The river cascades down a sheer, slippery cliff of black rock, guarded by dragons who never sleep. The water is cold death. It is unapproachable. Psyche stands at the base of the cliff, paralyzed by the vertigo, the noise, the sheer scale of the danger. But the eagle of Zeus swoops down from the clouds. He takes the flask in his talons. He flies into the center of the terror, dodging the dragons, dipping the flask into the freezing torrent, and returns it to her. She learns that sometimes, you cannot climb the mountain. You must take the high perspective to touch the source of death.

Finally, the fourth task. The descent. Venus hands her a small box. "Go to the Underworld. Go to Persephone, the Queen of the Dead. Ask her for a drop of her beauty ointment. I am weary from dealing with you. I need to refresh my face."

Psyche descends. She finds the vent in the earth. She walks past Cerberus, the three-headed dog, paying him with a honey cake to keep his jaws shut. She pays the grim ferryman Charon with a coin held in her mouth. She walks past the grasping hands of the dead who beg for her help, learning the hardest lesson of all: the ability to say "no" to pity in order to complete the mission. She reaches the Queen. Persephone, silent and pale, fills the box. Psyche returns, climbing the long, dark stair back to the light, her lungs burning for air.

She has succeeded. She has done the impossible.

But she is still human. As she stands in the sunlight, holding the box, a thought comes. A thought born of insecurity. "I am ragged. I am worn. I have walked through hell. My husband will not love me like this. I should take a little of the beauty for myself."

She opens the box.

There is no beauty inside. It is a trick. Inside is the Sleep of the Underworld. A cold, Stygian vapor rises up and enters her nostrils. It is not death, but a coma of absolute stillness. She falls to the ground, a corpse in everything but name.

But Eros has recovered from his burn. He has been watching from the window of his mother's palace. He sees her fall. He can bear it no longer. He escapes, flying faster than he has ever flown. He finds Psyche sleeping the sleep of the dead. He wipes the sleep from her face and puts it back in the box. He pricks her gently with one of his arrows, just enough to wake the blood.

"You almost died of curiosity again," he whispers.

He lifts her up. He carries her to Olympus. He appeals to Zeus himself. Zeus smiles and gives her the cup of Ambrosia. She drinks. The mortal clay is burned away. She ceases to be merely Psyche. She becomes a goddess. They are wed, and in time, they have a daughter. Her name is Pleasure.

III. The Reflection

The myth of Psyche and Eros is the master-map of the relationship between the human ego and the divine, and specifically, the torture required to transform attraction into love.

From Paradise to Consciousness

In the beginning, Psyche lives in a "Paradise of Unconsciousness." She is married to a god, but she is forbidden to see him. This corresponds to the initial phase of romantic love or spiritual awakening (Neumann 1956). We feel a presence. We feel connected. We are in the dark, carried by a force we do not understand. Everything is perfect because it is unexamined.

But the human soul (Psyche) cannot remain in the dark. The sisters represent the critical, cynical aspect of the intellect that demands empirical proof. "What is it? Is it safe?" The lighting of the lamp is the **Fall**, but it is a necessary fall. Psyche breaks the taboo because she needs **Consciousness**. She needs to *see* who she loves. Lacan would suggest that the lamp represents the intrusion of the **Gaze**. In the dark, Eros is pure feeling, pure fantasy. When the light hits him, he becomes an object. The drop of oil that burns him is the pain of objectification. We often burn our lovers when we try to force them to fit into our mental image, when we bring the harsh light of our analysis onto their fragile mystery (Lacan 2015).

Eros flees because the divine cannot be held by the possessive ego. It must be free.

The Four Tasks: The Labor of Love

Psyche's search for Eros is the process of **Individuation**. She can no longer just "be" beautiful; she must *do* the work. The four tasks represent the development of the four functions required to integrate the feminine principle (Von Franz 1980).

1. **Sorting the Seeds (Intuition/The Unconscious):** The pile of mixed seeds is the chaos of our emotions and drives. The ego cannot sort this mess. The ants represent the autonomic nervous system or the deep, instinctive wisdom of the body. When we are overwhelmed, we must stop thinking and let the "ants" (the intuition) do the work. We must trust that the order is already there.

2. **The Golden Fleece (Sensation/Patience):** The rams are the aggressive, solar libido. To approach them directly is to be destroyed by the intensity of desire or power. The reed teaches Psyche the power of the *via negativa*. Do not fight the energy when it is high. Wait. Gather the gold (wisdom) from the briars after the energy has passed. It is the lesson of timing and indirect approach.

3. **The Styx Water (Thinking/Perspective):** The waterfall is the overwhelming flux of life and death. To fill the cup, Psyche needs the Eagle (the symbol of Zeus/Spirit). She needs to detach. She needs to take a bird's-eye view. Sometimes, to deal with an emotional torrent, we need the distance of the intellect to dip the cup without being drowned.

4. **The Box of Beauty (Feeling/The Shadow):** This is the descent into the unconscious. She must face the Shadow (Persephone). She must learn to say "no" to the distractions (the grasping dead). But her failure at the end is crucial. She opens the box because she wants to be beautiful *for him*. It is a moment of vanity, yes, but also of supreme vulnerability. She collapses. This suggests that the ego cannot complete the journey alone. We can do the work, we can sort the seeds, but in the end, we need Grace. Eros must come to wake us up.

The Sleep of the Underworld

Heraclitus famously declared that "Hades and Dionysus are the same" (Hillman 2007). This paradox suggests that the realm of death and the god of indestructible life are two sides of the same coin. Psyche's "sleep" is not merely a failure; it is a Dionysian immersion. Dionysus is the god of excess, of the breaking of boundaries, and of the *Zoé* that flows through all things (Kerenyi 1976). By opening the box, Psyche is overwhelmed by an excess of essence that the limited ego cannot process, appearing as a death-like trance.

However, this collapse is structurally necessary. One cannot become immortal (a goddess) while holding onto the rigid defenses of the mortal ego. This "death" is the dissolving of the chrysalis. As Edgar Herzog writes, "To open oneself to death is to accept the aspect of 'becoming', that is, of transformation, which is the very stuff of life, and to realize that the human condition transcends itself" (Herzog 1998). It is only from this state of total surrender that Eros can wake her, not as a master waking a servant, but as a god waking a goddess.

The Sacred Marriage

The ending is not just a wedding; it is an apotheosis. Psyche drinks the ambrosia. She becomes immortal. This means that the soul, having gone through the trials of trust, patience, perspective, and death, is finally strong enough to sustain a union with the divine without being destroyed by it (Apuleius 1996).

They give birth to a daughter named **Pleasure** (Voluptas). Yet, this is not the fleeting pleasure of the senses. It is the deep, abiding joy that arises only after the soul has dared to violate the boundaries of the known. Psyche had to transgress. She had to light the lamp, and she had to open the box. Voluptas represents the truth that spiritual wholeness requires the integration of the transgressive impulse. As Georges Bataille suggests, the sacred and the erotic are intimately bound by the violation of limits. Pleasure is not the absence of tension, but the fruit of a necessary violation of the ego's boundaries in service of a higher union (Bataille 1986). It is the harmony that arrives only after the conflict has been exhausted.

Integration Practice: The Lamp and the Oil

Ask yourself: Where are you holding the lamp too close?

- Identify a relationship or a passion where you are demanding total clarity. Are you trying to analyze your partner to death? Are you trying to force a mystery to explain itself?
- Notice the drop of hot oil. That is your anxiety manifesting as control. When you demand to "know" everything, you burn the connection.

Practice: The next time you feel the urge to interrogate a feeling or a person, blow out the lamp. Sit in the dark with the uncertainty. Trust the touch, trust the feeling, and let the other person remain a subject, not an object of your investigation.

IV. References

- **Apuleius, L.** (1996). *The Golden Ass.* (P.G. Walsh, Trans.). Oxford: Oxford University Press.
- **Bataille, G.** (1986). *Erotism: Death and Sensuality.* San Francisco: City Lights Books.
- **Herzog, E.** (1998). *Psyche and Death.* Dallas: Spring Publications.
- **Hillman, J.** (2007). *The Dream and the Underworld.* New York: Harper & Row.
- **Jung, C. G.** (1982). *Aspects of the Feminine.* Princeton: Princeton University Press.
- **Kerenyi, C.** (1976). *Dionysos: Archetypal Image of Indestructible Life.* Princeton: Princeton University Press.

- **Lacan, J.** (2015). *Transference: The Seminar of Jacques Lacan, Book VIII.* (B. Fink, Trans.). Cambridge: Polity Press.

- **Neumann, E.** (1956). *Amor and Psyche: The Psychic Development of the Feminine.* Princeton: Princeton University Press.

- **Von Franz, M. L.** (1980). *The Golden Ass of Apuleius: The Liberation of the Feminine in Man.* Boston: Shambhala.

5 MARS: THE WARRIOR AND THE DRIVE

Archetype: Aggression, Separation, Willpower, Severing
Myth: Tyr Binding Fenrir (Norse)

I. The Context: The Knife That Separates

In our modern psychological lexicon, Mars often suffers from a reputation almost as bad as the planet's rugged, rusty surface. We associate it with war, rage, and toxic aggression. We see it as the red haze that descends when we lose control. But this is Mars in its shadow form (Moore & Gillette 1990). In its essence, Mars is the principle of **Separation**.

Before a thing can be loved (Venus), it must be distinct from everything else. Mars is the knife that cuts the umbilical cord. In this sense, it embodies the Lacanian *Nom-du-Père* (Name-of-the-Father), the symbolic function that intervenes to separate the subject from the fusional union with the mother, allowing the child to become an individual (Lacan 2006). It is the force of will that says "I am this, and I am not that." It is the energy of the *Drive* (*Trieb*) that pushes the seedling through the hard crust of the earth. Without Mars, the ego remains a soup, undifferentiated and powerless.

To understand the high cost of this power, we turn to the stark, frozen landscapes of Norse mythology. We look not to Thor, the thunderous brawler, but to **Tyr**, the original god of war and justice (Sturluson 2005). Tyr teaches us that the true work of the Warrior is not killing, but binding. And he teaches us that to bind the chaos of the world, one must be willing to pay a price in flesh (Crossley-Holland 1980).

II. The Myth

Let the breath leave your body in a long, slow exhale, carrying with it the tension of the day. As the air empties out, I want you to imagine cold. Not the damp, seeping cold of a winter rain, but the sharp, clarifying cold of the North. The air is thin and crystalline. It smells of pine resin and snow. You are standing in a valley of ancient stone, the roots of the world twisting beneath your feet like petrified veins.

The gods are gathered here. The Aesir. They are beings of immense power, radiant and strong, but today they are not laughing. They are afraid. You can smell the copper tang of their fear on the wind.

In the center of the circle stands the source of their terror. It is a wolf. Fenrir. He is not a normal beast. He is the offspring of Loki, the Trickster, and the giantess Angrboda. He has grown too fast. Yesterday he was a pup; today he is the size of a bull; tomorrow he will be large enough to swallow the sun. His fur is blacker than the space between stars. His eyes burn with an intelligence that is devoid of mercy. His jaw hangs open, drooling saliva that burns the grass where it falls. This is not just an animal. It is a hunger that never ends.

The gods know a prophecy. They know that at the end of time, at Ragnarok, this wolf will kill Odin, the All-Father. He will devour the wisdom of the world. They must bind him. They must contain the aggression before it consumes reality.

But how do you bind a force that grows stronger with every struggle?

They tried force. They forged a heavy iron chain called Leding. They challenged Fenrir to a game of strength. The wolf laughed, a low rumble that shook the mountains. He let them bind him. He stretched his muscles, and the iron snapped like dry twigs. The gods forged a second chain, Dromi, twice as heavy, twice as strong. Fenrir let them drape it over his shoulders. He shook himself, and the metal shattered into dust.

Force cannot bind such power. Resistance only makes it stronger.

Desperate, Odin sent a messenger to the Svartalfheim, the realm of the dark elves, the master craftsmen of the underworld. "Make us a fetter that cannot break," he commanded.

The dwarves did not use iron. They used the impossible. They gathered six ingredients: the sound of a cat's footfall, the beard of a woman, the roots of a mountain, the sinews of a bear, the breath of a fish, and the spittle of a bird. They forged these non-things into a ribbon called ***Gleipnir****.*

It looks like nothing. It is as smooth and soft as silk, light as a spiderweb. It is a paradox: a binding made of things that do not exist.

The gods return to the island of Lyngvi. They show Fenrir the ribbon. "This?" the wolf sneers. "There is no glory in breaking a piece of silk. I refuse."

But the gods goad him. "Are you afraid, Fenrir? Do you fear a ribbon?"

The wolf's eyes narrow. He smells the trap. The instinct is sharper than any thought. "This ribbon is made of treachery," he growls. "I will not let you bind me. Unless..."

He looks at the circle of gods. He looks at Thor with his hammer, at Odin with his spear. He looks for a sign of good faith. A pledge.

"I will let you bind me," Fenrir says, his voice a rasp of gravel and blood. "But only if one of you places his hand in my mouth. As a pledge that this is no trick."

Silence falls over the valley. It is a terrible, heavy silence. The gods look at their hands. Hands are the tools of their power. Hands hold the sword, the hammer, the scepter. To lose a hand is to lose agency. To be maimed is to be less than a god.

Odin steps back. Thor steps back. The price is too high.

Then, Tyr steps forward.

Tyr is the god of Law. He is the god who separates right from wrong. He is calm. He does not boast. He walks up to the massive, hulking beast. He looks into the abyss of the wolf's throat, where rows of teeth glint like obsidian knives. He smells the rot of digested meat. He knows exactly what is going to happen. There is no hope of escape. There is no trick to save him.

Slowly, deliberately, with the steady rhythm of a man accepting his fate, Tyr raises his right hand. The hand of the sword. The hand of the oath. He places it between the massive jaws. He lays his wrist on the wolf's tongue.

The wolf closes his mouth gently, just enough to feel the pulse of the god. He waits.

The other gods move quickly. They wrap the silken ribbon, Gleipnir, around the wolf's neck and legs. They tie the knots.

Fenrir begins to struggle. He expects the silk to snap. But the impossible ribbon holds. It hardens. The harder he kicks, the tighter it bites. He thrashes, he howls, he realizes he is trapped. The panic of the caged beast rises in him. He bites down.

There is a sickening crunch. The sound of bone snapping. Blood sprays onto the white snow, vivid and shocking.

Tyr does not scream. He stands pale and still as the wolf tears his hand from his wrist. He watches his own blood stain the ground. He watches the gods cheer as they anchor the chain to a great stone and drive it deep into the earth. The chaos is bound. The world is safe. The sun will rise tomorrow.

But Tyr stands apart. He wraps his bleeding stump in his cloak. He has saved the world, but he will never hold a sword again. He has paid the price for order.

III. The Reflection

The myth of Tyr and Fenrir provides a brutal, necessary corrective to our fantasies of the "Hero." We often imagine the Hero as the one who kills the monster and rides home in triumph (Campbell 1964). But Mars, in his most mature aspect, is not the killer. He is the **Binder**. And the act of binding requires a sacrifice that the ego is terrified to make.

The Problem of the Drive

Fenrir represents the **Drive** (*Trieb*). In Lacanian psychoanalysis, the Drive is distinct from biological instinct. Instinct has a rhythm; it is satisfied when the animal eats or sleeps. The Drive, however, is a constant pressure (Lacan 1978). It is the "wolf" in the psyche that always wants *more*. It is the excess of energy that does not fit into the polite structures of society. It is pure, unbound aggression and desire.

The myth shows us that you cannot bind the Drive with force (the chains of iron). When we try to repress our aggression with sheer willpower ("I will not be angry," "I will be good"), the Drive only grows stronger. The shadow swells. The "Nice Guy" who represses his Mars eventually snaps, just as Leding snapped (Hillman 1975).

The only thing that binds the Drive is **Gleipnir** (the Symbolic). The ribbon is made of "non-things" because the Symbolic order (Language, Law, Culture) is immaterial. We are bound not by iron chains, but by words, by promises, by social contracts. It is the "No" of the Father that structures the psyche.

The Castration Complex and the Law

The central image of the myth is the hand in the mouth. In psychoanalytic terms, this is the acceptance of **Symbolic Castration**. To enter civilization, to become a functioning subject, we must give something up. We cannot have total, unbound enjoyment (*Jouissance*). We cannot be the wolf who eats the world. We must accept a limit.

Tyr represents the Ego that is willing to accept this limit for the sake of order. The hand is the instrument of *grasping*. It represents our capacity to take what we want, to wield power directly. By sacrificing the hand, Tyr sacrifices the fantasy of omnipotence. He accepts that he cannot "have it all."

This is the difference between a boy and a man, or the immature and mature Mars.

- The **Immature Mars** (Fenrir) wants to devour everything. It accepts no limits. It is the rage of the toddler who screams when he is told "no."

- The **Mature Mars** (Tyr) understands that power requires limitation. He gives up the "right hand" (immediate gratification/violence) to establish the "Law" (binding the chaos).

As Jungian analyst Edward Edinger notes, "The creation of consciousness requires a sacrifice of the unconscious wholeness" (Edinger 1985). We cannot remain in the blissful, animal state of the wolf. We must be maimed into humanity (Jung 1967).

The Courage of Separation

Mars is the planet of separation. In the myth, Tyr separates himself from the other gods. While they stand back in fear, he steps forward. This act of stepping forward is the essence of **Willpower**. Willpower is not about forcing the world to bend to you. It is about the willingness to endure pain for a chosen value. Tyr does not hope to save his hand. He knows the cost. He chooses the meaning of the act over the integrity of his body.

In our lives, we often face "Fenrir moments": situations where a chaotic force (an addiction, a toxic relationship, a destructive rage) threatens to swallow our world. We try to bind it with iron (rules, diets, force), and we fail. The myth suggests that to truly bind the chaos, we must put our hand in the mouth. We must make a sacrifice.

- To bind the chaos of alcoholism, one must sacrifice the "hand" that holds the glass (the social ritual, the coping mechanism, the "friend" that alcohol was).

- To bind the chaos of a toxic relationship, one must sacrifice the hand that holds tight onto the other (the fear of being alone, the economic consequences, the uncertainty).

It hurts. It leaves a stump. But it saves the world.

Integration Practice: The Sword and the Hand

Ask yourself: What is the "Wolf" in your life right now?

- Identify the force of excess or aggression that feels like it is growing too large to contain. Is it a temper? A hunger? A compulsion?

- Notice how you have been trying to bind it. Have you been using "iron chains" (sheer repression, harsh self-talk)? Notice how the wolf breaks them.

- Ask: What is the "Hand" I must sacrifice to bind this? What pleasure, what habit, or what fantasy of wholeness must I give up to establish order?

Practice: When you feel the Drive rising, visualize Tyr. Imagine placing your hand in the mouth of the urge. Acknowledge the pain of saying "no" to yourself. Do not try to pretend it doesn't hurt. Accept the pain as the price of your sovereignty.

IV. References

- **Campbell, J.** (1964). *The Masks of God: Occidental Mythology.* New York: Viking Press.

- **Crossley-Holland, K.** (1980). *The Norse Myths.* New York: Pantheon Books.

- **Edinger, E.** (1985). *Anatomy of the Psyche: Alchemical Symbolism in Psychotherapy.* La Salle: Open Court.

- **Hillman, J.** (1975). *Re-Visioning Psychology.* New York: Harper & Row.

- **Jung, C. G.** (1967). *Symbols of Transformation* (Collected Works of C.G. Jung, Vol. 5). Princeton: Princeton University Press.

- **Lacan, J.** (1978). *The Four Fundamental Concepts of Psycho-Analysis* (Book XI). New York: W. W. Norton & Company.

- **Lacan, J.** (2006). *Écrits: The First Complete Edition in English.* (B. Fink, Trans.). New York: W. W. Norton & Company.

- **Moore, R., & Gillette, D.** (1990). *King, Warrior, Magician, Lover: Rediscovering the Archetypes of the Mature Masculine.* San Francisco: HarperSanFrancisco.

- **Sturluson, S.** (2005). *The Prose Edda.* (J.L. Byock, Trans.). London: Penguin Classics.

6 JUPITER: THE KING AND EXPANSION

Archetype: The Father (benevolent), Expansion, Meaning, Hybris
Myth: The Legend of Oghuz Khagan (Turkic)

I. The Context: The Architecture of Belief

If Mars is the knife that separates the ego from the mother, Jupiter is the force that expands that separated ego into a world. In astrology (Tarnas 2006) and depth psychology, Jupiter represents the principle of **Expansion**, *Joviality*, and the establishment of a moral or social order. He is the King who does not rule by force alone, but by the weight of his presence and the beneficence of his law.

However, the shadow of Jupiter is inflation. It is the risk of the ego mistaking itself for the god, a condition Jung termed the "Mana Personality" (Jung 1966). To wield the power of Jupiter is to hold the scepter of authority without being crushed by its weight.

To explore this massive, regal energy, we turn to the steppes of Central Asia and the foundational myth of the Turkic peoples: **The Legend of Oghuz Khagan** (Ögel 1993; Lewis 1974). Unlike the tragedies of the Greeks or the trickery of the Chaco, this is a story of vertical power within a specific cosmological order (Bazin 1991). It is the story of a man who is born supernatural, who conquers the four corners of the world not just to own them, but to organize them under a single, divine law (*Töre*). It is a study in how meaning is anchored in a chaotic universe.

II. The Myth

Let your gaze soften and expand, as if you are looking out over a horizon that has no end. Imagine the smell of sagebrush and dry earth. You are standing on the vast, open Steppe.

Above you is the Eternal Blue Sky, Tengri, a dome of infinite depth. There are no walls here. There are no ceilings. There is only the wind that travels from the rising sun to the setting moon.

In the tent of Ay-Khagan (Moon Khan), a child is born. But this is not an ordinary birth. The infant's face is blue like the sky, his mouth is red like fire, and his eyes are almandine, glowing with a dark, terrifying vitality. He is born fully formed, radiating a heat that makes the air in the yurt shimmer.

From the moment he draws his first breath, he does not cry like a human infant. He speaks. His voice is deep, resonating from a chest that already feels too broad for a cradle. He pushes away his mother's breast, rejecting the white, sweet milk of infancy. He demands the food of warriors. He calls for raw meat, dripping with life, and red wine, fermented and strong. He consumes them with a terrifying hunger. He does not grow by the slow turning of seasons. He grows by the hour. His limbs stretch and thicken with a cracking sound, like young trees bursting through stone. In forty days, he is no longer a child. He stands upright. In forty nights, he is riding, wrestling wild horses to the ground with his bare hands. His body is not smooth skin. It is covered in thick, coarse hair like the coat of a grey wolf. He is Oghuz. He is not a man to be raised. He is a force of nature that cannot be domesticated.

The land is trembling under the weight of a shadow. A monster plagues the forest, a Rhino-beast of such primordial violence that it devours horses and men alike, leaving nothing but crushed bone and silence in its wake. The people are paralyzed by a terror that lives in the gut, a heavy, cold stone of fear. But Oghuz does not hide. He does not shrink. As you imagine him walking into the dense, dark green of the forest, you might feel a straightening in your own spine, a resonance with courage that knows no hesitation. He carries a spear of iron and a shield of bronze, and he moves with the inevitable rhythm of a glacier.

He finds a clearing. He ties a deer to a willow tree as bait. And then, he waits. He does not fidget. He stands in the center of the danger, breathing in the scent of pine and damp earth, becoming as still as the trees themselves. Notice the silence that falls before the storm... the way the birds stop singing... the way the air grows heavy and thick with expectation.

Then, the earth begins to shake. It is a low frequency vibration that you can feel in the soles of your feet. The beast charges. It crashes through the undergrowth, a juggernaut of grey muscle and singular, murderous intent. It smells of old blood and wet fur. The ground shudders with every stride. Most men would run. Most men would close their eyes against the impending impact. But Oghuz stands his ground. He roots himself into the soil, becoming immovable, becoming the anvil against which the hammer will break.

He does not use a trick. He does not use magic. He uses the direct application of will. Just as the horn, a lance of bone capable of piercing stone, descends to impale him, Oghuz strikes. It is a single, perfect motion. The spear finds the gap. The shield deflects the crushing weight. Sword in hand now, and with a roar that drowns out the monster's own cry, he severs the head. The massive body collapses, sliding into the dirt with a sound like a falling mountain.

The silence returns, but it is different now. It is the silence of victory. Oghuz does not leave. He sits on the carcass of the beast. He uses the body of the terror as his throne. He wipes the black blood from his blade, his eyes burning with the cool fire of dominance. He has looked the biological threat in the eye and unmade it. He is the Master of the Wild.

But a King needs more than strength. He needs a Queen. He needs a connection to the divine.

One night, Oghuz stands alone under the canopy of the world. He is praying to Tengri, the Eternal Blue Sky. The silence of the steppe is absolute, a vacuum waiting to be filled. As he looks up, the darkness splits open. A beam of light descends, not golden like the sun, but a deep, electric blue: the color of the zenith, the color of the infinite. It strikes the earth with a soundless impact, brighter than the moon, brighter than the day.

Inside this pillar of blue fire sits a girl. She is not of the earth. She does not sit on the ground; she floats within the luminescence. Her face is etched with the geometry of stars. She is so beautiful that the breath leaves Oghuz's lungs. When she smiles, the horizon seems to expand. When she laughs, the blue sky laughs with her, a sound like wind rushing through high mountain passes, clearing the clouds. She is the Anima of the Sky, the celestial principle made flesh.

Oghuz approaches her. He does not take her by force; he takes her by destiny. He makes her his wife. From this union of the Earth-King and the Sky-Maiden, three sons are born. They are not merely children; they are principles of light. The first is Gün (Sun), radiant and burning. The second is Ay (Moon), cool and reflective. The third is Yıldız (Star), distant and guiding. These are the children of the Sky.

Time passes, and Oghuz rides out again. This time, he does not look up; he looks down. He travels deep into the ancient forest, where the canopy is so thick that the sun is a mere memory. In the center of this silence lies a lake, dark and still as a mirror of obsidian. And in the middle of the lake stands a massive tree. It is old, its bark peeling, its trunk hollowed by the slow, relentless work of time and rot. Yet, from this decay, life is blooming.

Inside the hollow of the tree sits another girl. She is not made of light; she is made of substance. Her skin has the rich, pale glow of birch wood. Her eyes are not the electric blue of the zenith, but the deep, teeming blue of the sky reflected in deep water. Her hair flows down her back like a river seeking the sea, heavy and wet. She smells of wet earth, of moss, of the fertile darkness where seeds crack open.

Oghuz wades into the water. He understands that while the Sky gives inspiration, the Earth gives structure. He takes her as his wife. From this union of the King and the Earth-Maiden, three more sons are born. They are the architects of the physical world. The first is Gök (Sky), representing the atmosphere that hugs the earth. The second is Dağ (Mountain), the spine of the land, immovable and high. The third is Deniz (Sea), the depth that surrounds and holds the continents. These are the children of the Earth.

With his lineage secured, Oghuz declares himself Khagan of the World. "I am your Khan," he tells his people. "Let us take bows and shields. Let the Wolf be our guide."

One morning, as the dawn bleeds crimson across the steppe, a presence manifests at the edge of the camp. It is the Gökbörü, the Blue-Maned Wolf. It stands taller than a warhorse, its fur shimmering with the strange, metallic light of the spirit world. It does not howl. It does not hunt. It simply turns its massive head to look at Oghuz, locks eyes with the King, and then turns West.

Oghuz understands. This is the vector of destiny. He mounts his horse. His army, a river of steel and leather, mounts behind him. They follow the Wolf. It is a campaign of absolute expansion, a centrifugal force pushing the boundaries of the known world.

They ride into the lands of the setting sun. They cross deserts where the sand burns the hooves of their horses. They penetrate the lands of eternal darkness, where the sun never rises and the cold bites like iron teeth. They ride across the frozen seas of the North, the ice groaning beneath the weight of their ambition. They do not stop until there is no more land to conquer.

But Oghuz does not merely burn and kill. He is not a storm that destroys; he is an architect who builds. When he defeats a tribe, he does not erase them. He incorporates them. He gathers the scattered, nameless peoples of the earth under a single banner of the Wolf. He gives them identity.

To the people who invented the cart with high wheels, he says: "You are the Kangly." To the people who flocked to him like a river joining the sea, he says: "You are the Uyghur." He imposes language upon the chaos of the steppe. He transforms a mob into a nation, a brawl into a hierarchy. He creates an empire that stretches from where the sun rises to where it sets, becoming the Axis Mundi, the center pole around which the world now turns.

But Oghuz grows old. His hair turns to silver. He has the world, but he needs to ensure the Order survives his death. He needs a Law.

His wise counselor, Ulugh Turk, dreams of a Golden Bow stretching from the East to the West, and three Silver Arrows flying towards the North. Oghuz understands. This is the command of Tengri.

He sends his three elder sons, the children of the Sky, to the East. They find a Golden Bow buried in the earth. He sends his three younger sons, the children of the Earth, to the West. They find three Silver Arrows.

They return to the great banquet. Oghuz Khagan takes the Golden Bow. He breaks it into three pieces and gives them to the elder sons. "You are the Bozok (Broken Bows)," he says.

"You shall rule the center. You shall be the Kings."

He gives the Silver Arrows to the younger sons. "You are the Üçok (Three Arrows)," he says. "You shall be the ambassadors. You shall guard the borders."

In this final act, Oghuz does the most difficult thing a conqueror can do. He replaces his own will with the Law. He establishes the hierarchy of the feast, creating the ***Töre****. He decrees the* ***Oron****, the sacred place where each lineage must sit, so that no man need fight for his status. He decrees the* ***Ülüş****, the rightful share of the meat. He assigns the shoulder to the Khan, the hip to the warrior, the rib to the counselor. He maps the body of the animal onto the body of the state.*

He transforms his raw power into a structure that can endure time. He ensures that even when his heart stops beating, his Order will continue to hold the roof of the world up.

Then, the work is done. The golden banquet fades. The voices of his sons and his people drift away like smoke.

Oghuz Khagan stands up from his throne. He does not look back at the empire he built. He looks only at the flap of his tent, which is fluttering in the wind. He walks out. He has expanded the self until it covers the horizon. He has pinned the world down with his arrows.

Outside, the night is absolute. But there, waiting in the starlight, is the Blue-Maned Wolf. It has returned. Oghuz smiles, his silver hair catching the light of the stars he once conquered. He closes his eyes, steps forward into the silence, and the Blue Wolf guides him home, across the threshold of the last horizon.

III. The Reflection

The legend of Oghuz Khagan is a masterful depiction of the **Jupiterian** stage of psychological development. If Mars is the energy that fights to separate the ego, Jupiter is the energy that expands that ego to encompass and organize the world. It is the archetype of the **King**.

The Mana Personality and Inflation

Oghuz is born with supernatural features: blue skin, wolf hair, rapid growth. In Jungian terms, this represents the **Mana Personality** (Jung 1966). Mana is a Melanesian word describing a supernatural force or "charge." The Mana Personality occurs when the ego integrates the contents of the collective unconscious and becomes charged with a terrifying, numinous power.

We see this in individuals who have "Jupiterian" charisma (great leaders, gurus, or captains of industry). They seem larger than life. They have enormous energy. But the danger, as Jung warned, is **Inflation**. The ego may believe *it* is the source of this power, rather than the vessel for it (Edinger 1972). Oghuz avoids the catastrophe of inflation because he constantly refers his power back to **Tengri** (The Sky God). He follows the Blue Wolf (an instinctual guide from the unconscious) rather than his own whims. A true King knows he is a subordinate to a higher principle. A tyrant believes he is the principle.

The Master Signifier and the Symbolic Order

From a Lacanian perspective, the most critical moment of the myth is not the battles, but the finding of the **Golden Bow** and **Silver Arrows**. The world before Oghuz is a place of scattered tribes and chaos (The Real). Oghuz creates a civilization by introducing **Master Signifiers** (*Signifiants Maîtres* or S1).

The Golden Bow operates as the **Master Signifier**. It is an arbitrary object that Oghuz invests with absolute authority. By breaking the bow and distributing it, he acts as a **Quilting Point** (*Point de capiton*). Just as a button holds the stuffing of a mattress in place, the Bow stops the "sliding of signifiers" inherent in the chaotic steppe. It fixes meaning. He says: "Because you hold this piece of the bow, you are the Bozok. You sit *here*. You eat *this* part of the meat."

This is the function of the **Symbolic Order** (Lacan 2007). It quilts the sliding reality into a stable social fabric. It stops the chaos. The *Töre* (Law) is not natural; it is constructed. But it must *feel* inevitable for society to function. Oghuz acts as the *Name-of-the-Father*, the authority that lays down the law which regulates enjoyment and lineage. He transforms "meat" into "a feast with protocols." He transforms "fighting" into "hierarchy."

The Psychology of Expansion

Jupiter asks us: "How big is your world?" Oghuz travels until he touches the boundaries of the earth. Psychologically, this represents the need for the Self to expand its territory. We must integrate the "children of the Sky" (our spiritual, intuitive ideas) and the "children of the Earth" (our practical, grounded realities). However, expansion without structure is just obesity (physical or psychic). Oghuz does not just conquer; he **organizes**. He names the tribes. In our own lives, Jupiterian energy is the urge to learn a new language, to travel, to start a business, or to build a philosophy. But this expansion only becomes wisdom when we can find the "Golden Bow", the central organizing principle, or *Axis Mundi* (Eliade 1959), that ties all our experiences together into a coherent whole.

The Return to the Source

Finally, the myth concludes with a profound image of release. Oghuz does not die in a bed; he walks out to meet the **Blue Wolf (Gökbörü)**. In Jungian psychology, the Wolf acts here as a **psychopomp**, a guide of souls that mediates between the conscious world and the deep unconscious. The Wolf appeared at dawn to lead the libido outward into conquest (expansion). Now, at twilight, it returns to lead the libido back to the source (involution).

This return is crucial. Oghuz leaves *after* establishing the Law but *before* he becomes a tyrant. By following the Wolf away from his throne, he avoids the trap of the "Negative Senex" (the rigidity of the old king who refuses to yield). He surrenders his inflated ego back to **Tengri** (The Self). He proves that he is not the owner of the power, only its vessel. He completes the solar cycle: rising, shining, and voluntarily setting into the dark.

Integration Practice: The Throne and the Border

Ask yourself: Where are you abdicating your throne?

- Identify an area of your life where you feel chaotic, small, or disorganized. Is it your finances? Your creative work? Your household?
- Imagine yourself as Oghuz Khagan. You are not a victim of this chaos; you are the Khan who has not yet established the Law.
- **The Expansion:** What do you need to learn or acquire to master this domain?
- **The Law:** What "Golden Bow" (rule or structure) do you need to establish? Is it a schedule? A budget? A code of conduct?

Practice: Choose one chaotic area. Write down three Laws for that area. Do not frame them as chores; frame them as Imperial Decrees. "From this day forth, the Law of this house is..." Feel the weight of the Scepter as you write it.

IV. References

- **Bazin, L.** (1991). *Les Systèmes chronologiques dans le monde turc ancien.* Budapest: Akadémiai Kiadó.
- **Edinger, E.** (1972). *Ego and Archetype: Individuation and the Religious Function of the Psyche.* New York: G.P. Putnam's Sons.
- **Eliade, M.** (1959). *The Sacred and the Profane: The Nature of Religion.* New York: Harcourt, Brace & World.

- **Jung, C. G.** (1966). *Two Essays on Analytical Psychology* (Collected Works of C.G. Jung, Vol. 7). Princeton: Princeton University Press.

- **Lacan, J.** (2007). *The Other Side of Psychoanalysis: The Seminar of Jacques Lacan, Book XVII.* (R. Grigg, Trans.). New York: W. W. Norton & Company.

- **Lewis, G.** (1974). *The Book of Dede Korkut.* London: Penguin Classics.

- **Ögel, B.** (1993). *Türk Mitolojisi (Kaynakları ve Açıklamaları ile Destanlar).* Ankara: Türk Tarih Kurumu Basımevi.

- **Tarnas, R.** (2006). *Cosmos and Psyche: Intimations of a New World View.* New York: Viking.

7 SATURN: THE SENEX AND THE LIMIT

Archetype: The Wise Old Man, Time, Melancholy, Structure, Authority
Myth: Cronus Devouring His Children (Greek)

I. The Context: The Weight of the World

We now leave the expansive, golden plains of Jupiter and cross the threshold into the dark, enclosed gravity of the seventh sphere. In the ancient cosmology, Saturn was the *Ultima Thule*, the furthest planet visible to the naked eye. He was the Gatekeeper of the Sphere of Fixed Stars, the boundary between the known solar system and the terrifying infinity of the cosmos beyond.

Saturn is the archetype of the **Limit**.

In astrology, he is known as the "Great Malefic," the bringer of cold, hunger, isolation, and death (Klibansky et al. 1964). In alchemy, he is associated with Lead (*plumbum*), the heaviest and basest of metals, and the state of *Nigredo* (blackening), the decomposition that must occur before any transformation can take place (Edinger 1985). He is the god of Time (*Chronos*), not in the sense of the flowing river, but in the sense of the inevitable entropy that grinds mountains into dust.

Yet, despite this grim reputation, Saturn is arguably the most critical archetype for the development of a soul. As James Hollis suggests, without Saturn, we have no structure, no spine, and no reality (Hollis 1994). We remain eternal children (*Puer Aeternus*), flying high on wax wings, melting in the sun because we refuse to touch the ground. Saturn is the force that pulls us down. He is the gravity that forces the spirit to incarnate in the heavy, painful, beautiful world of matter.

To understand this archetype, we must look into the darkest mirror of Greek mythology , primarily recorded in Hesiod's *Theogony* (Hesiod 2006), particularly with the alternative ending (Graves 1955). We must examine the story of **Cronus**, the Titan King who did not want to rule the world, but to stop it. It is a story of a father so terrified of the future that he ate it. It is the story of the heavy hand of the past, the "Negative Senex" who refuses to die, and the terrible price the soul must pay to escape the belly of the father.

II. The Myth

I invite you now to let the breath sink low in your body. Let it drop from the chest to the belly, and from the belly to the hips, feeling the pull of the earth beneath you. Imagine that your bones are becoming heavy, dense, and ancient, like veins of iron running through a mountain. The air around you grows cold and still. It is the silence of a library at midnight, or the silence of a winter forest where the snow absorbs every sound. You are entering the domain of the Old King, a place where time slows down and thickens, like sap turning to amber.

But before there was the Old King, there was the Scream.

The story begins with a crime, a violation that echoes through the deep structure of the cosmos. In the beginning, the Sky (Uranus) lay heavy upon the Earth (Gaia). Imagine a sky that is not a distant dome, but a pressing, suffocating weight. A sky of solid lead. He would not let her breathe. He would not let her children, the Titans, emerge from the womb of the earth into the light. He hated them. He pushed them back down, stuffing them into the dark, cramped caverns of their mother's body. Can you feel the pressure? The claustrophobia of potential that is forbidden to exist? Gaia groaned in agony, a sound like shifting tectonic plates.

She forged a sickle. Not of shining bronze, but of gray flint: cold, jagged, and older than metal. It was a tool made of the earth itself, sharp with an ancient, geological anger. She begged her sons to help her. Only one dared.

Cronus. The youngest. The coldest. He did not do it for justice. He did not do it for love. He did it for power, and because the crushing weight had made him hard. He took the flint sickle, its edge hungry for separation. He waited in the ambush of the earth's folds, a shadow within a shadow. And when his father, the Sky, descended to copulate with the Earth, a vast, overwhelming presence blocking out all light, Cronus struck.

He reached out with his left hand, the sinister hand, the hand of the unconscious, and seized his father. With his right hand, he drove the flint sickle through the genitals of the god. It was a violent, severing act. A sound like the tearing of the fabric of reality. He severed the connection between Heaven and Earth, creating the space in which we now live. He cast the severed parts into the sea, where they foamed and birthed Venus, but that is a different story. This story is about the blood that fell on the earth, heavy drops that birthed the Furies, the spirits of vengeance who never forget.

Cronus took the throne. He became the King. He freed his brothers and sisters, the Titans, into the new space between earth and sky. But he did not free the monsters, the Cyclopes and the Hundred-Handed Ones. He left them locked in the dark of Tartarus. He was a liberator only of what looked like him, what he could control. He established the Golden Age. The poets tell us it was a time of peace, but it was the peace of a frozen lake. It was a time when milk flowed in rivers and honey dripped from oaks, a world of effortless abundance, but it was also a time without time. Nothing changed. Nothing died. Nothing was truly born. It was a static, frozen perfection, held in place by the iron will of a King who had killed his own source to stop the flow of generation.

But the curse of the father is that he becomes what he killed. As Uranus lay dying, bleeding his power into the earth, he prophesied with a voice like thunder rolling in a distant cave: "You, too, will be overthrown by your own child."

The prophecy burrowed into Cronus's mind like a cold worm in a sweet apple. It ate his sleep. It ate his peace. It turned the honey of the Golden Age into ash in his mouth. He looked at his wife, his sister Rhea, not with love, but with suspicion. He watched her belly swell with the first child, and he saw not new life, but his own ending.

And so began the great swallowing, the attempt to eat the future.

When Hestia was born, the first child, a goddess of the hearth, mild and kind, Cronus did not see a daughter. He saw a usurper. He took the infant from Rhea's arms. He did not strike her. He did not drown her. He opened his mouth, a cavern of ancient, wet darkness that smelled of old earth and time itself, and he swallowed her whole. Imagine the silence that followed. The warmth of the hearth swallowed into a cold void. He trapped her in the prison of his own body. He wanted to keep her "inside," under his control, forever.

Then came Demeter, the goddess of the harvest, carrying the scent of ripe grain and fertile soil. He swallowed her, burying the promise of growth within his own stagnation. Then Hera, the queen, radiant with authority. He swallowed her power into his own. Then Hades, the lord of the silent underground. Swallowing him was like swallowing a shadow, a piece of the night itself. Then Poseidon, the shaker of the earth, smelling of salt and the deep ocean. Cronus swallowed the sea, containing its vast, chaotic energy within his own rigid form.

Imagine the horror of Rhea. She is the Great Mother, the flow of life (Rheos), and she is married to the Great Stopper of Life. Every time she brings potential into the world, the structure of the past devours it. She watches her husband grow heavier, denser, his belly distended with the terrible weight of the five living gods inside him. He sits on his throne of black obsidian, unmoving, a mountain of a god, his eyes fixed on a horizon that never changes. He has stopped time. He has eaten the future, and it sits heavy in his gut.

Inside the belly of the father, it is not death. It is worse. It is stasis. The children are alive, but they cannot grow. They are suspended in the gastric juices of the old order, blinded by the darkness of his paranoia. They are conscious, but they have no agency. They are thoughts that cannot become actions. They are the depression of the soul that is trapped in the "way things have always been," unable to move forward or back.

Rhea is pregnant again. The sixth child. She feels the kick of this one inside her. It is different. It is stronger. It is electric. It is a pulse of raw, untamed energy. It is **Zeus**. *She cannot bear to lose him to the void. The instinct of life within her rebels against the rule of death. She flees to the island of Crete, to the wild, untamed edges of the world. She goes to the deep cave of Mount Dicte, the secret womb of the earth. There, in the damp, echoing dark, protected by the earth that birthed her husband, she gives birth to the storm.*

But she must return to Cronus. The law of the father demands it. She must present him with a child, or he will hunt her down and tear the world apart to find what she has hidden. She needs a decoy. A substitute for reality.

She finds a stone lying on the mountainside. A cold, hard, lifeless rock, rough to the touch, heavy with the weight of the earth. Notice its weight in your own hands as you imagine holding it. It has no pulse. It has no warmth. It is pure, unfeeling matter. Rhea wraps this stone in soft, white swaddling clothes, the raiment of a newborn. She holds it to her breast as if it were warm flesh, infusing the cold rock with the appearance of life. She returns to the throne room and presents it to the King.

Cronus does not look closely. He does not unwrap the bundle to touch the skin. He is blinded by his obsession with control, by the overwhelming need to silence the prophecy. He sees a bundle, and he sees a threat. He opens his terrible maw and swallows the stone. You can almost feel the heavy, cold object sliding down his throat, crashing into the pile of living, silent gods in his stomach. He feels the weight. He feels the fullness. He sighs, a sound like wind blowing through a desolate canyon. "It is done," he thinks. "I am safe. Time is stopped."

He has swallowed the **Omphalos**, *the center of the world. But he thinks he has swallowed his death.*

Meanwhile, in the cave on Crete, hidden from the all-seeing eye of the father, the true child grows. He is not raised in the golden palace. He is raised in the wild. He is nursed by a goat, Amalthea, drinking the rich, primal milk of instinct. He is guarded by the Kouretes, the armored dancers who clash their bronze spears against their shields in a rhythmic, hypnotic beat every time the baby cries, drowning out the sound of new life so the father on the distant mountain will not hear. This is the secret education of the soul: growing in the dark, fed by instinct, protected by noise and movement, hidden from the crushing judgment of the Senex until it is strong enough to stand.

Zeus grows. He integrates the power of the sky and the earth. But raw power is not enough to defeat the leaden weight of the past. Force alone cannot crack the density of Saturn. He needs strategy. He needs Cunning. He leaves the cave of his childhood and travels to the edge of the world, where the great river Oceanus encircles the earth. There, walking on the grey, shifting sands, he finds ***Metis****, the goddess of wisdom and prudent counsel.*

Metis is not like the other Titans. She does not have the solid, crushing presence of Cronus. She is fluid. Her eyes change color like the sea, shifting from gray to green to deep violet. She understands that the straight line of the sword is not always the path to victory. Zeus asks her for a weapon. He asks for a blade that can slice open the belly of a god. Metis shakes her head. Her voice is the sound of water lapping against rock, patient and eroding.

"You cannot cut the past open from the outside," she tells him. "The skin of the Father is too thick. If you strike him, he will only harden. To free your siblings, you must make him reject them from within. You must make the container refuse its contents."

She takes a clay cup. She does not fill it with nectar. She gathers herbs from the salt-marshes, plants that taste of bitterness and revolt. She mixes mustard seed and salt, elements that irritate, elements that cause the body to convulse. She brews a potion that is not a poison designed to kill, but an emetic designed to purge. It is the liquid essence of "No." It is the chemical agent of revolution. She hands the cup to Zeus. "Do not be a warrior yet," she whispers. "Be a servant. Be invisible. Feed him the thing he cannot hold."

Zeus disguises himself as a humble cupbearer. He ascends to the mountain of Othrys, where the Titans rule in their frozen majesty. He approaches the throne of his father. Cronus is old now, ancient beyond reckoning. His skin is like cracked leather, his eyes cloudy with eons of unchanging rule. He takes the cup from the young stranger. He does not recognize his own son. He does not taste the bitterness of the future in the wine. He drinks deep.

The potion works instantly. The stomach of the King convulses. The tectonic plates of his being begin to shift. The old order cannot hold the new life any longer. Cronus doubles over, groaning with an agony that shakes the foundations of the mountain. It is the pain of a world forced to change. He vomits.

First comes the Stone. It flies out of his throat, a cold, hard projectile of reality, crashing onto the earth at Delphi, marking the center of the new world. And then, with a rush of released pressure, come the children. They emerge fully grown, unharmed by their long stasis, their eyes burning with the light of their liberation. Poseidon bursts forth with the roar of the ocean, reclaiming the seas. Hades emerges with the silence of the grave, claiming the underworld. Hera, Demeter, Hestia - they stand beside their brother, a pantheon of differentiated powers, no longer a confused mass in the father's belly.

The war that follows, the Titanomachy, lasts ten immortal years. It is not a battle of armies; it is a collision of realities. Imagine the sound of the sky tearing open. It is a screeching, metallic rending that vibrates in your teeth. On Mount Othrys stand the Titans, vast and heavy, beings of stone and slow time. They throw mountains. You can feel the impact in the soles of your feet as boulders the size of cities slam into the earth, raising clouds of dust that choke the sun.

Opposing them on Mount Olympus are the new gods, the children of the vomit. They are faster. They are lighter. Zeus releases the Cyclopes from the dark, and in gratitude, they forge him the Thunderbolt. Can you smell the ozone? The air becomes thick and electric, the hair on your arms standing up as the atmosphere charges. When Zeus throws the bolt, it is not just light; it is a physical hammer of heat. It strikes the leaden shields of the Titans, melting them, turning the old, heavy structures into running slag.

But the Titans are stubborn. They are the past, and the past does not want to die. To break the stalemate, Zeus unleashes the ultimate terror: the Hecatonchires, the Hundred-Handed Ones. Imagine a being with fifty heads and one hundred arms, a hurricane of limbs. They pick up three hundred massive stones at once. They hurl them with a speed that turns the air to fire. It is a bombardment that eclipses the sky. The Titans are buried under the sheer volume of the new possibilities.

Finally, Zeus confronts his father. It is the meeting of Lead and Lightning. Cronus wields the sickle, the tool of separation, but he is slow, weighed down by his own gravity. Zeus wields the bolt, the tool of illumination. The strike is blinding. It sears the retina. The thunderbolt shatters the sickle. The heavy, suffocating silence of the Golden Age is broken by the roar of the new King.

Cronus falls. He is not killed (gods cannot die) but he is displaced. Zeus banishes him to the depths of Tartarus, the deepest pit beneath the earth, behind bronze gates, to be bound in chains for eternity. Or, as some gentler stories tell it, he is sent to the Isles of the Blessed, at the very edge of the world, to sleep forever in a golden cave, dreaming of a time that will never return.

The reign of Lead is over. The reign of Silver and Gold begins. But the Stone remains at Delphi, a cold, hard, permanent monument to the thing the father could not digest, the center around which the new world must turn.

III. The Reflection

The myth of Cronus is perhaps the most clinically accurate description of the **Negative Father Complex** and the archetype of the **Senex** (The Old Man) in its destructive mode. While Jupiter represents the "Good Father" who blesses and expands (as seen in the legend of Oghuz Khagan), Saturn represents the "Terrible Father" who curses and restricts.

The Saturnian Shadow and the Father Wound

James Hollis, in his seminal work *Under Saturn's Shadow*, uses this myth to map the specific wounding of men (and the animus in women) in patriarchal culture. Cronus represents the burden of the past. He is the father who has been wounded by his own father (Uranus) and unconsciously passes that wound down to his children.

The "swallowing" is a metaphor for **psychic consumption**.

- It is the father who imposes his own unlived life onto his son ("I wanted to be a doctor, so you must be a doctor").
- It is the father who competes with his child, subtly undermining their successes because he fears being surpassed (the prophecy).
- It is the father who is emotionally absent, forcing the child to live in the "belly" of his silence, waiting for a recognition that never comes.

When we are "in the belly of the father," we are in a state of **Saturnian depression**. We feel heavy. We feel that the walls are closing in. We feel that time is stuck. We have potential (we are gods, like Poseidon and Hera), but we have no agency. We are defined entirely by the structure that contains us (Hollis 1994).

The Alchemy of Lead: The Necessity of Nigredo

However, we must be careful not to simply demonize Saturn. In alchemy, Saturn corresponds to **Lead** (*Prima Materia*). Lead is heavy, dull, gray, and poisonous. But it is also the beginning of the work. You cannot make gold without lead.

Psychologically, Saturnian energy manifests as **Melancholy** or depression. In our modern, Jupiterian society, we are obsessed with "growth," "happiness," and "expansion." We pathologize sadness. We want to be manic (Icarus). Saturn reminds us that without the weight of lead, we have no substance. The "swallowing" period is the **Nigredo**, the dark night of the soul. It is a time of incubation. Just as the wine must ferment in the dark cask, the soul must sometimes sit in the belly of the beast, cut off from the light, to develop density and gravity. A person with no Saturn is flighty, ungrounded, and eternally immature (*Puer Aeternus*). A person with too much Saturn is crushed, cynical, and paralyzed. The goal is to "vomit the stone": to emerge from the depression not by escaping it, but by passing through it and finding the solid object (the Self) that cannot be destroyed (Hillman 2005).

This leads us to the central axiom of the Great Work: the path to the Alchemical Gold (*Aurum Non Vulgi*) begins solely with Saturnian Lead. The alchemists insisted that the philosopher's stone was found *in sterquiliniis* (in the dunghill), meaning in the rejected, heavy, and despised parts of our experience. This concept parallels modern leadership theory, specifically the idea of the "crucible." As Bennis and Thomas (2002) argue, true leadership does not emerge from ease, but from intense, often traumatic experiences, which they call "crucibles", that force the individual to examine their values and emerge stronger. Just as the alchemist finds gold in the filth, the leader finds their authority in the very experiences they wished to avoid.

Saturn is not the enemy of the Gold; he is its container. The density of lead is actually a form of concentrated energy waiting to be released. By enduring the pressure of Saturn, the coal of the ego is slowly compressed into the diamond of the Self. We do not transcend our limitations by flying away from them (Jupiter/Icarus); we transcend them by going deeper into them until we find the hidden light at the core of the darkness.

The Lacanian "Père-Jouissance" (The Obscene Father)

From a Lacanian perspective, Cronus offers a terrifying glimpse of the **Superego**. We often think of the Superego as the "moral conscience" that tells us to be good. But Lacan identified a darker side to this agency: the obscene, ferocious Superego that commands enjoyment and punishes the subject for failing to enjoy, or conversely, enjoys the punishment itself (Zižek 2006).

Cronus is the **Primal Father of the Horde** (referencing Freud's *Totem and Taboo*). He is the father who monopolizes all *Jouissance* (enjoyment). He keeps all the women (Earth/Rhea) and all the children for himself. He refuses to allow the Symbolic Order (the exchange of women, the circulation of power) to function. He creates a blockage. The "Law" of Saturn is not the regulating Law of the Symbolic (which allows desire to flow, like traffic lights); it is the crushing Law of the Real (which stops all movement). It is the voice that says "NO" not to protect you, but because it enjoys saying "NO." The stone that Rhea feeds him is the **Object *a*** - the indigestible piece of the Real that chokes the Superego. It is the one thing the tyrant cannot assimilate, operating as ***Das Ding* (The Thing)**, the unsymbolizable remainder that breaks the cycle of total consumption (Lacan 1992).

The Titanomachy: Winning with the Repressed

The war itself offers a strategic map for overcoming the Saturnian complex. Why does Zeus win? Not because he is morally superior, but because he is structurally inclusive. Cronus lost because he repressed the "monsters" (the Cyclopes and the Hundred-Handed Ones) locking them in Tartarus because they did not fit his orderly aesthetic. He tried to maintain a purity of form.

Zeus wins because he descends into Tartarus and liberates the repressed. In Jungian terms, this is the **integration of the Shadow**. To defeat the rigid, paralytic depression of the Senex, the ego (Zeus) must reclaim the "ugly" or chaotic parts of the self that were previously rejected.

- **The Cyclopes** represent the "Single Eye" of intuition and the power to forge the **Thunderbolt** (Sudden Insight). Depression is often broken not by gradual logic, but by a flash of insight that shatters the dark.

- **The Hecatonchires** (Hundred-Handed Ones) represent the sheer, chaotic multiplicity of life-energy.

The lesson of the Titanomachy is that you cannot defeat the oppression of the Father using only the Father's rules. You need the raw, elemental power of the "monsters" he locked away. You need your rage, your messiness, and your wildness to forge the bolt that breaks the stagnation. This is the retrieval of what Robert Bly calls the "Wild Man" and Clarissa Pinkola Estés calls the "Wild Woman" - the instinctual, un-sanitized vitality that lies at the bottom of the psyche's dungeon (Bly 1990; Estés 1992). Without this primal energy, the intellect remains a cupbearer, not a King.

The Stone at Delphi: Establishing the Center

The climax of the myth is the vomiting of the **Omphalos** (The Navel Stone). Zeus places this stone at Delphi, the center of the Greek world. This is a profound symbol of integration. The very thing that was used to trick the father (the cold, hard reality) becomes the cornerstone of the new consciousness. This teaches us that our "stone," our trauma, the hard lump of pain we carried in the dark, the thing our father couldn't digest, is not trash. It is the center. It is the foundation upon which we build our own temple. We do not get rid of our Saturnian wounds; we objectify them, place them in the center of our psychic geography, and build a new order around them.

Integration Practice: The Emetic Potion

Ask yourself: What have you swallowed that isn't yours?

- **Identify the Ingested Beliefs:** Sit quietly and feel the weight in your "belly." Are you carrying beliefs about money, imposed clothing choices, worthiness, or duty that actually belong to your father (or mother/culture)? "You must work hard to be loved." "Men don't cry." "Security is more important than joy."

- **The Stone Test:** Look at these beliefs. Are they warm living flesh (your own truth)? Or are they cold stones wrapped in swaddling clothes (deceptions you were fed)?

- **The Emetic:** What is the truth that this system cannot digest? Is it your creativity? Your queer identity? Your desire for rest?

Practice: Visualize the Stone. Imagine taking it out of your body, vomiting it up, not in violence, but in relief. Place it on the ground in front of you. Say to it: "This is a fact. This happened. But it is not *me*. It is the foundation I stand on, not the weight I carry."

IV. References

- **Bennis, W. G., & Thomas, R. J.** (2002). Crucibles of Leadership. *Harvard Business Review*, 80(9), 39–45.

- **Bly, R.** (1990). *Iron John: A Book About Men*. Reading, MA: Addison-Wesley.

- **Edinger, E.** (1985). *Anatomy of the Psyche: Alchemical Symbolism in Psychotherapy*. La Salle: Open Court.

- **Estés, C. P.** (1992). *Women Who Run with the Wolves: Myths and Stories of the Wild Woman Archetype*. New York: Ballantine Books.

- **Freud, S.** (1913). *Totem and Taboo: Resemblances Between the Psychic Lives of Savages and Neurotics*. (A. A. Brill, Trans.). New York: Moffat, Yard and Company.

- **Graves, R.** (1955). *The Greek Myths*. London: Penguin Books.

- **Hesiod.** (2006). *Theogony*. (M.L. West, Trans.). Oxford: Oxford University Press.

- **Hillman, J.** (2005). *Senex and Puer: An Aspect of the Historical Present.* Putnam: Spring Publications.

- **Hollis, J.** (1994). *Under Saturn's Shadow: The Wounding and Healing of Men.* Toronto: Inner City Books.

- **Klibansky, R., Panofsky, E., & Saxl, F.** (1964). *Saturn and Melancholy: Studies in the History of Natural Philosophy, Religion, and Art*. London: Nelson.

- **Lacan, J.** (1992). *The Seminar of Jacques Lacan, Book VII: The Ethics of*

Psychoanalysis 1959–1960. (D. Porter, Trans.). New York: W. W. Norton & Company.

- **Zižek, S.** (2006). *How to Read Lacan.* London: Granta Books.

8 URANUS: THE AWAKENER AND REBELLION

Archetype: The Rebel, Insight, Disruption, Promethean Fire
Myth: Prometheus Stealing Fire (Greek)

I. The Context: The Lightning Strike

We move now from the heavy, leaden gravity of Saturn to the electric, erratic orbit of the eighth sphere. In the structure of the psyche, if Saturn is the walls of the castle, Uranus is the lightning bolt that shatters the tower.

Uranus is the planet of the unexpected. It is the only planet in our solar system that spins on its side, rolling like a ball rather than spinning like a top. This astronomical anomaly perfectly mirrors its psychological function. It is the archetype of the **Outsider**, the Rebel, and the genius who perceives reality from a perpendicular angle to the status quo.

While the planet is named after Ouranos (the Sky Father), the archetypal energy it carries is far better described by the figure of **Prometheus**, the Titan who defied Zeus to bring fire to humanity, a narrative immortalized by the playwright Aeschylus (Aeschylus 2009). Richard Tarnas, in his defining work on archetypal cosmology, argues persuasively that Uranus is the planetary expression of the Promethean impulse (Tarnas 2006). This is the impulse to transcend boundaries, to defy authority for the sake of a higher truth, and to introduce the "fire" of higher consciousness into the dark, cold world of biological survival.

But the fire comes at a cost. The Awakener does not bring peace. He brings disruption. He creates a rupture in the fabric of reality that can look like madness, trauma, or revolution. To understand Uranus, we must walk the path of the thief who stole from the gods not for greed, but for love of the future.

II. The Myth

I invite you now to find a particular kind of stillness in your body. It is not the heavy, leaden sleep of the earth we explored before. It is different. Let your spine lengthen. Let your eyes soften, but keep your senses sharp, like an animal listening for a crackling twig in the deep woods. It is an alert stillness, a state of high potential energy, where you are ready to move, ready to see, ready to wake up.

And as you hold this tension, this quiet vibration in your nerves, let your attention begin to drift backward against the flow of time. Watch the lights of the modern world flicker and die. Watch the cities dissolve into iron, the iron into stone, the stone into mud. Let the roads roll back up like carpets. Let the farms turn back into forests. Drift past the warmth of history, past the fires of the great civilizations, past the very first hearth that was ever lit.

Go deeper. Go back to the time before heat. You are entering the First Age. The air here is thin and sharp. It bites at the skin. It smells of ozone and ancient ice. There is no sun here, only a gray, perpetual twilight that stretches out over a landscape of jagged rock and freezing mist. Can you feel the cold? It is a physical weight. It presses against your eyes. It seeps into the marrow. It is a world waiting for a spark.

Imagine a world without fire. It is a world of perpetual twilight. The sun rises and sets, but its heat does not linger. When the dark comes, it is absolute. It is a physical weight that presses against the eyes. The wind howls across the plains, stripping the heat from the skin of the creatures who huddle in caves. These creatures are humans, but they are not yet fully human. They are shivering animals. They eat their meat raw, tearing at bloody sinew with flat teeth. They sleep in piles to keep from freezing. They live in a state of constant, trembling fear. They fear the leopard. They fear the storm. But mostly, they fear the cold that seeps into the marrow and stops the heart.

High above, on the peaks of Olympus, far removed from the shivering mud, there is a different reality. Here, there is light. Not the pale, watery light of the moon, but a rich, golden radiance that bathes everything in eternal noon. There is warmth here, a luxurious, radiant heat that seeps into the stones of the palaces and the skin of the immortals. The gods sit around hearths of eternal flame, fires that do not smoke, fires that do not need to be fed. They recline on couches of cloud and ivory. They eat cooked meat, the savory smoke of the burnt offerings rising from the world below as a pleasing, savory incense. They drink nectar that tastes of sunlight and immortality. They are wrapped in the comfort of their own power, oblivious to the chattering teeth in the darkness below.

They are indifferent to the shivering things below. Zeus, the King, the Structure, the current expression of Saturnian authority, has decreed that fire belongs only to the divine. He believes that if the clay creatures below possess the spark, they will forget their place. They will become arrogant. They will challenge the order of the cosmos.

But there is one among the immortals who cannot turn away. Prometheus. He is a Titan, older than the Olympians, cut from a rougher, more ancient stone. His name means "Foresight," but it is more than just seeing the future. It is the curse of seeing the potential within the unformed. He looks down from the heights, his eyes piercing through the cloud cover, and he does not see mud-creatures. He sees the ghost of what they could become. He sees the latent geometry in their minds, the dormant poetry in their tongues, the cities of steel and glass sleeping in the ore of the mountains. He sees a species that could rival the gods, if only they had the catalytic spark. He looks at their shivering bodies, and he feels a pain that is alien to the other gods. He feels empathy. He feels the terrible waste of a universe where consciousness remains frozen in the dark.

A tension builds in his chest. It is the high-voltage hum of rebellion. It is the refusal to accept a law that lacks compassion.

He devises a plan. It begins with a trick at the feast of Mekone. Picture the scene. The air is thick with the smoke of roasting meat, a scent that makes the mouth water and the belly tighten. Gods and mortals stand on opposite sides of a great stone table. The tension is palpable. It is a negotiation of power disguised as a dinner. Prometheus steps forward as the carver. He has slaughtered a great ox, dismantling the heavy beast with surgical precision. Now, he must divide the shares.

He creates two piles. In the first, he places the choice cuts, the tenderloin, the rich muscle, the parts that sustain life. But he wraps them in the ox's stomach lining. It is gray, glistening with slime, smelling faintly of digestion and offal. It looks repulsive. It looks like waste. In the second pile, he heaps the bare, dry bones. But over this calcified emptiness, he drapes thick layers of pure white fat. It shines in the sunlight, smooth and opulent, promising richness. It is a lie wrapped in beauty.

He asks Zeus to choose. The King of the Gods looks down from his high seat. He sees the glistening white pile. His eyes, accustomed to the perfection of Olympus, are drawn to the aesthetic of the fat. He judges by the surface. With a greedy hand, he points. "That one," he thunders. "That is the portion of the gods."

Zeus reaches out. His fingers sink into the soft, cool fat. He peels it back, expecting succulent meat. Instead, there is a dry, hollow sound. Click. Clack. The fat falls away to reveal nothing but the white, jagged cage of the skeleton. The mockery is absolute. The trick is revealed not in words, but in the tactile reality of the empty bones. Zeus looks across the table at Prometheus, who stands with a small, dangerous smile. The King's face does not turn red with anger. It turns white with a cold, administrative fury. He realizes the structure of his authority has been hacked.

In retaliation, Zeus does not strike Prometheus immediately. He strikes the creatures Prometheus loves. He looks at the shivering humans who are now feasting on the good meat hidden in the offal. "You may have the meat," he pronounces, his voice like a closing door. "But you shall eat it in the dark." He withdraws fire from the earth. He sucks the heat out of the air. The hearths go cold. The torches sputter and die. The night becomes absolute, a suffocating blanket of ice that descends to choke the world.

Prometheus knows what he must do. He knows the punishment for defying the King. He looks at the future, and he accepts the price.

He takes a stalk of giant fennel. The plant is green and hollow, with a pith that burns slowly, holding heat without consuming the shell. It is a vessel. He begins the ascent. He does not fly on wings of grace; he climbs with the heavy, stubborn weight of earth. Feel the grit of the granite tearing at his fingertips. Feel the burning ache in the muscles, the lactic fire that builds with every upward pull. He hauls his massive frame up the sheer face of Olympus, finding purchase on ledges of ice that shatter under his grip. The air grows thin, starving the lungs, forcing him to gasp for every breath in the rarefied atmosphere. The wind turns razor sharp, a physical blade that slices through his tunic, stripping the heat from his skin and howling with a voice that sounds like a warning from the void. He climbs past the heavy, wet clouds. He climbs past the highest arc of the eagles, entering a silence so profound it rings in the ears. He crosses into the forbidden zone of the ether, where the sky turns from blue to a deep, bruised violet, and the light becomes a blinding, sterile white that offers no comfort, only exposure.

He reaches the rim of the sun. Perhaps, he creeps into the workshop of Hephaestus, the smith. If not, he waits for the Chariot of the Sun to pass. Imagine the heat. It is not the comforting warmth of a campfire. It is a roaring, blinding radiation. It is the energy of a nuclear explosion. It is terrifying. Prometheus shields his eyes. He extends the fennel stalk. He thrusts it into the wheel of the burning chariot.

A spark catches. The dry pith inside the green stalk ignites. He pulls it back. He shields the tiny, glowing ember with his hand. He holds the seed of civilization in a hollow reed.

Then, he turns and runs. The descent is not a walk; it is a controlled fall. Gravity grabs him, pulling him down from the ether into the heavy atmosphere of earth. He leaps over crevasses that would swallow a mortal whole, his feet finding purchase on shifting scree that clatters into the void. He is a blur of motion, a streak of green fennel and golden fire cutting through the monochrome gray of the twilight world. The wind screams in his ears, a high-pitched keen of protest as he violates the boundary between the divine and the profane. He creates his own lightning, not from the sky, but from the speed of his transgression. He rushes down the slopes, his chest heaving, protecting the fragile ember as if it were his own heart. Finally, the air grows thick and damp. He smells the stale odor of unwashed bodies and fear. He reaches the caves of the shivering men. Without a word, without a pause for breath, he tosses the glowing stalk onto a pile of dry, brown leaves.

At first, there is only smoke. Then, a crackle. Then, the miracle. Orange tongues of flame lick the air. The humans recoil in terror. It bites. It creates its own wind. But Prometheus shows them how to feed it. He shows them that this hungry spirit can be tamed.

The transformation is instantaneous. The darkness is pushed back. The cave becomes a home. The raw meat becomes a feast. The cold is banished. Around the fire, community is born. Language is forged in the circle of light. The clay creatures look up, and the fear is gone from their eyes. In its place is a new light. The light of consciousness. They are no longer animals. They are gods in the making.

High on Olympus, Zeus stands on the balcony of the world. He looks down. The earth, which should be a void of obedient darkness, is changed. It is speckled with lights. Thousands of tiny, flickering orange stars mirror the cold, white stars of the heavens. He sees the fires dotting the dark earth like reflected stars, and he understands instantly what has happened. The barrier between the divine and the mortal has been breached.

His fury is not the red, hot anger of a brawler. It is something far more terrifying. It is cold. It is administrative. It is the anger of a grand architect who sees a structural flaw that threatens the integrity of the entire edifice. He does not scream. He does not throw thunderbolts at the ants below. He calculates. He understands that this is not just a theft; it is an infection. Consciousness has leaked. If the mortals have fire, they will soon have technology. They will have art. They will have war. They will eventually look up and question why they should serve.

He turns his gaze to the perpetrator. He does not just kill Prometheus. Death is too simple for a Titan. Death is a release. Zeus needs an example. He needs a living monument to the cost of rebellion. He designs a torture that is also a symbol. It must be cyclical, like the seasons. It must be agonizing, like the birth of consciousness. It must be eternal, like the order he intends to maintain.

He calls upon Hephaestus, the divine smith, the god who is himself broken, to do the work of breaking another. He commands him to forge chains of adamantine, a metal so hard it does not reflect light, but absorbs it. Hephaestus hesitates. He knows Prometheus. He respects the intellect of the rebel. But the command of Zeus is not a request. It is a law of nature. Hephaestus pumps the bellows. He heats the unforgiving metal until it glows with a dull, malevolent red. He shapes the links, each one a testament to the inescapable weight of authority.

They drag Prometheus to the Caucasus. It is the end of the world. There are no trees here. There is no soft grass. There is only vertical rock and a wind that never stops screaming. It is a place of absolute exposure. They slam him against the cliff face. The rock is freezing against his back, a stark contrast to the fire he once held. Hephaestus raises his hammer. The sound of the first strike rings out like a bell tolling for the death of freedom. Clang. The shackle closes around the left wrist. Clang. The right wrist is bound. The metal bites into the flesh, cold and final.

But the binding is not enough. Zeus demands fixation. He wants the rebel pinned, unable to shift, unable to turn away from the consequences of his vision. Hephaestus takes a wedge of diamond-hard steel. He places the point against the Titan's chest, right over the sternum, the bone that guards the heart. He raises the hammer high. With a grunt of effort, he drives the wedge down. It pierces the skin. It cracks the bone. It drives through the chest cavity and sinks deep into the granite behind him. Prometheus is no longer just on the mountain. He is part of the mountain. He is fused with the rock of suffering.

And then, the bird comes.

It begins as a speck in the blinding zenith of the sun, a black flaw in the perfection of the light. It grows larger. The sound arrives before the shadow, a rushing noise like a tearing sail. It is the Eagle of Zeus, the manifest will of the Sky Father, descending to reclaim what was stolen. It does not circle. It dives.

It impacts the Titan's chest with the force of a falling stone. The breath is driven from Prometheus's lungs. The talons, curved obsidian hooks as long as daggers, sink into the pectoral muscles, anchoring the bird to the living rock of the god's body. Prometheus gasps, his eyes wide, staring up into the golden, unblinking eye of the predator. There is no hatred in that eye. There is only the cold, mechanical efficiency of the law.

The beak descends. It is not jagged. It is polished, sharp as a surgeon's scalpel, designed for precise excavation. It tears the skin of the abdomen. It parts the muscle. It pushes past the ribs with a sickening crack. It seeks the center. It finds the liver, the dark, blood-rich seat of vitality and passion. And then, it eats. It tears the organ of life from the body of the rebel in wet, ragged strips. The eagle feeds not on meat, but on the very source of the Titan's defiance, consuming the fire of his biology to feed the cold authority of the sky.

The pain is absolute. It is not merely the sharp sting of the cut; it is the deep, nauseating ache of violation as the organ is ripped from its moorings. It is the primal panic of the body being hollowed out while the mind remains terrifyingly lucid. He gasps, arching his back against the unforgiving stone, but the chains hold fast. He screams, but the sound is swallowed by the wind. And yet, the cruelty of his punishment is not death. It is life. Prometheus is immortal. He cannot escape into the oblivion of the grave. He is forced to remain present, fully conscious, witnessing his own evisceration.

When the sun finally sets, dipping below the jagged horizon, the bird takes flight, leaving him bloody and gaping in the twilight. The temperature plummets. The cold wind of the Caucasus turns into a physical assault, freezing the blood on his chest into dark, jagged icicles. The frost acts as a brutal cauterization, sealing the edges of the wound with ice. And then, in the silence of the night, the true horror begins. Because he is a Titan, his body obeys the imperative of wholeness. The flesh begins to knit together. He feels the strange, crawling sensation of cells multiplying at a supernatural rate. The liver regrows, swelling back into the cavity, heavy and whole. The skin stretches over the wound, sealing him back into perfection. He heals not for relief, but for repetition. He lies there in the dark, whole and terrified, watching the eastern horizon, waiting for the first gray light that signals the return of the wings.

And in the morning, the Eagle returns.

This is the cycle. The theft, the light, the binding, the tearing, the healing. Prometheus hangs on the cliff for thirty thousand years. He does not scream apologies. He does not beg for mercy. He looks out over the world he saved, watching the fires of humanity burning in the distance, and he endures. He pays the rent for our consciousness with his own agony.

III. The Reflection

The myth of Prometheus is the defining narrative of the **Uranian** archetype. It maps the transition from a stable, unconscious order (Saturn/Cronus or established Zeus) to a chaotic, higher consciousness. It teaches us that "waking up" is essentially a transgressive act.

The Lightning Bolt of Insight

Uranus is the planet of **Sudden Insight**. In the myth, fire is not developed slowly through evolution; it is stolen and delivered in a flash. This corresponds to the psychological experience of the *Satori* moment, the epiphany, or what Jung called the "synchronistic event" (Jung 1960). It is a vertical strike that cuts across the horizontal linearity of our lives.

According to Astrology, when Uranus transits a sensitive point in the natal chart (Hand 1976), or when we encounter this archetype in life, we experience a sudden shattering of our "Persona" (the mask we wear for society). In this story, Zeus (having become the Ruler) represents the Ego-Structure: the rules, the safety, the predictable hierarchy. Prometheus represents the **Self** demanding liberation. The fire he steals is **Consciousness** itself. As Jung noted, the expansion of consciousness always feels like a crime against the unconscious. It feels like a theft. To know more than your tribe, to see further than your father, is to commit an act of hubris. It isolates you. The "fire" burns the one who carries it (Jung 1967).

The Trauma of the Real

From a Lacanian perspective, the Promethean act can be understood as an encounter with the **Real**. In *The Ethics of Psychoanalysis*, Lacan (1992) posits that the Moral Law exists to keep us at a safe distance from ***Das Ding*** **(The Thing)**—the traumatic, forbidden core of the Real. By stealing the fire, Prometheus violates this distance. He transgresses the Law of the Father (Zeus) to grasp the forbidden object, thereby rupturing the Symbolic order.

Zeus had a law: "No fire for humans." This law created a stable, albeit cold, reality. Prometheus introduces an element that the law cannot contain. This is the definition of **Trauma**. Trauma is often described, notably by Freud, as a fire that burns through the protective shield of the psyche (Freud 1920). But in this myth, the trauma is the *cause* of humanity. We are the species that was traumatized into intelligence. The fire forced us to adapt, to speak, to build. The rupture of the Real is what forces the Symbolic to expand (Žižek 1989).

The Liver and the Eagle: The Cost of Anxiety

The most haunting image of the myth is the torture: the daily eating of the liver. Why the liver? In Greek medicine, the liver was the seat of the passions and vitality. It is the organ of blood and life. The Eagle represents the **Spirit** (Zeus/Air/Sky). The liver represents the **Body/Instinct**. The punishment of Prometheus describes the inevitable tension of the awakened human condition: **Anxiety**. To possess fire (consciousness) is to be separated from the animal state of blissful ignorance. We can foresee the future (Prometheus means "Foresight"), which means we can foresee our own death. We are bound to the rock of material existence (the body), yet we are tormented by the Spirit (the Eagle) that pecks at our vitals.

The regeneration of the liver suggests that this suffering is chronic. It is the "maintenance cost" of brilliance. Many Uranian individuals, specifically geniuses, rebels, and innovators, suffer from a nervous system that is constantly being "eaten" by the intensity of their own insights. They experience high anxiety, nervous exhaustion, or the feeling of being "pinned" by a reality that is too slow for their minds. As Marie-Louise von Franz points out in her work on the *Puer Aeternus*, the danger of the Promethean flight is that one becomes stuck in the realm of the spirit (the heights) and experiences the body only as a place of torture (Von Franz 2000). Prometheus represents the archetypal image of human existence defined by suffering and consciousness (Kerenyi 1997).

The Necessity of the Rebel

Despite the agony, Prometheus does not apologize. This is the crucial Uranian lesson. There are times in the life of the psyche when disobedience is a moral imperative. If we remained under the rule of Zeus, we would still be shivering in the dark. The "Good Child" (the compliant ego) stays cold. It is only the "Bad Child" (the rebel) who brings the warmth. James Hillman argues that the "pathologizing" function of the psyche (the symptoms, the rebellions, the breakdowns) is actually the soul trying to wake us up (Hillman 1975). The breakdown is the breakthrough. The theft of fire is the crime that makes us human.

Integration Practice: The Lightning Rod

Ask yourself: Where are you too obedient?

- **Identify the Cold Cave:** Look at your life. Where are you shivering? Where are you starving for "fire" (passion, truth, change) because you are afraid of upsetting the "Gods" (family expectations, social norms, the inner critic)?

- **The Fennel Stalk:** What acts of rebellion are you fantasizing about? It doesn't have to be a grand revolution. It might be the theft of time (taking an hour for yourself), the theft of voice (speaking a forbidden truth), or the theft of identity (changing your career).

- **Accept the Eagle:** Understand that if you steal the fire, there will be anxiety. The Eagle will come. Do not try to medicate the Eagle away immediately. Recognize the anxiety as the heat of the fire you stole.

It is proof that you are alive.

Practice: Perform one "micro-rebellion" today. Break a small rule that makes no sense. Wear something that doesn't "fit." Say "no" to an obligation. Feel the heat of the disruption.

IV. References

- **Aeschylus.** (2009). *Prometheus Bound.* (J. Scully & C.J. Herington, Trans.). Oxford: Oxford University Press.

- **Freud, S.** (1920). *Beyond the Pleasure Principle*. (J. Strachey, Trans.). London: The Hogarth Press.

- **Hand, R.** (1976). *Planets in Transit: Life Cycles for Living*. Atglen, PA: Whitford Press.

- **Hillman, J.** (1975). *Re-Visioning Psychology.* New York: Harper & Row.

- **Jung, C. G.** (1960). *The Structure and Dynamics of the Psyche* (Collected Works of C.G. Jung, Vol. 8). Princeton: Princeton University Press.

- **Jung, C. G.** (1967). *Symbols of Transformation* (Collected Works of C.G. Jung, Vol. 5). Princeton: Princeton University Press.

- **Kerenyi, C.** (1997). *Prometheus: Archetypal Image of Human Existence*. Princeton: Princeton University Press.

- **Lacan, J.** (1992). *The Seminar of Jacques Lacan, Book VII: The Ethics of Psychoanalysis 1959–1960*. (D. Porter, Trans.). New York: W. W. Norton & Company.

- **Tarnas, R.** (2006). *Cosmos and Psyche: Intimations of a New World View*. New York: Viking.

- **Von Franz, M. L.** (2000). *The Problem of the Puer Aeternus*. Toronto: Inner City Books.

- **Žižek, S.** (1989). *The Sublime Object of Ideology*. London: Verso.

9 NEPTUNE: THE MYSTIC AND DISSOLUTION

Archetype: The Dreamer, Illusion, Addiction, Oneness, The Ocean
Myth: Tren Tren and Kai Kai Vilu (Mapuche/Argentina)

I. The Context: The Solvent of the Soul

We have traveled far from the central fire of the Sun and the solid walls of Saturn. We have even moved beyond the electric disruption of Uranus. We now cross the threshold into the deep, dark blue of the ninth sphere. Here, the boundaries of reality do not just break. They dissolve.

Neptune is the planet of the mist. In the astrological and psychological model, it represents the universal solvent (Greene 1996). It is the force that erodes the hard structures of the ego, the logic of Mercury, and the laws of Saturn, returning all things to a primal, undifferentiated unity. It is the archetype of the Mystic, the Dreamer, and the Addict.

While Uranus liberates us through a sudden shock (the lightning bolt), Neptune liberates us through a slow, seductive erosion (the flood). It whispers that separation is an illusion. It promises a return to the womb, a return to the ocean of oneness where the burden of being an individual "I" is finally washed away. This is the source of our highest spirituality and compassion, for in Neptune we realize we are all one. Yet it is also the source of our deepest madness, deception, and escapism, for in Neptune we lose the ability to distinguish what is real from what is dreamed.

To understand this watery, overwhelming power, we must turn our gaze to the Southern Cone of South America. We look to the mythology of the Mapuche people of Argentina and Chile (Cooper 1946; Faron 1964). Their cosmology is not built on the static pillars of Olympus. It is built on a dynamic, terrifying balance between the forces of water and the forces of earth (Bacigalupo 2007).

It is the story of **Tren Tren and Kai Kai Vilu**, the dual serpents who constantly unmake and remake the world. This myth teaches us that the only defense against the flood of the unconscious is the elevation of the spirit.

II. The Myth

I invite you to gently close the door on the dry, brittle world of logic you inhabit during the day. Allow your body to settle into the chair, feeling the pull of gravity shift. It is no longer a weight pressing you down. It is a depth opening up beneath you, a soft invitation to sink. Let your breathing slow down, matching the rhythm of a distant, slow-moving tide. Imagine the air in the room changing texture. It becomes heavy, thick with moisture, cooling against your skin like a mist rising from a deep lake at dawn. You can smell it now. It is the scent of impending rain, the rich, dark odor of wet earth and river mud, the electric ozone that hangs in a valley right before the storm breaks. The sharp outlines of your thoughts begin to blur, softened by this rising fog. You are leaving the clear, harsh light of the mind where everything is separate and distinct. You are drifting into the wetlands of the soul where everything touches everything else.

Let your mind travel south now. Drift away from the noise of the cities, leaving behind the grids of concrete and glass. Float over the vast, flat silence of the pampas, where the horizon stretches out forever, an ocean of grass that ripples under a restless wind. You are moving toward the bottom of the world, toward the ancient, wind-swept forests of Patagonia and the Araucanía. The air here changes. It becomes cleaner, colder, carrying the scent of damp moss and thousand-year-old wood.

Here, the earth thrusts upward in violent protest against the sky. The mountains are not gentle hills. They are sharp spines of granite, jagged teeth of the Andes biting into the clouds. They stand as the ultimate symbol of the solid, of that which refuses to move. They are the bones of the planet exposed to the elements, dark and unforgiving.

But against this hardness crashes the sea. And this is not a gentle, tropical sea. It is a cold, gray monster that never sleeps. It heaves with the weight of the Southern Ocean, crashing against the cliffs with a rhythmic, thunderous violence that pulverizes stone into sand. The world here is defined by this eternal tension between the solid and the fluid. It is a war of attrition between the rock that wants to remain and the water that wants to dissolve.

In the beginning of this cycle, there was peace. The Mapuche people lived in the valleys. They fished in the rivers. They harvested the piñones from the great Araucaria trees. They forgot that the earth is not a dead thing. They forgot that the land and the sea are not objects, but living, breathing wills. They became complacent. They stopped listening to the machi, the shamans who speak the language of the wind. They believed that the ground beneath their feet was permanent.

But nothing in the domain of Neptune is permanent.

Now I want you to let your mind sink. Let it drop past the surface where the light plays, down into the heavy, silent blue. Go deeper still. You are descending into the bathypelagic zone, the midnight zone. Here, the weight of the water presses against you like a thick, cold blanket, holding you, surrounding you from all sides. The darkness is not just an absence of light. It is a presence. It is a crushing, velvet blackness where the sun has never touched, a place of absolute, ancient cold that seeps into the bones and slows the pulse. And in this silence, which is louder than any noise, you might begin to sense a vibration. It is not a sound you hear with your ears. It is a tremor you feel in your fluids. Something stirs. A massive, slumbering will is shifting its coils in the deep, displacing the water with a slow, tectonic power.

It is Kai Kai Vilu. To call it a serpent is to diminish it. It is a geological event made of flesh and malice. Its body coils through the trenches like a mountain range in motion, vast enough to encompass the horizon. The scales are not merely dark. They absorb the faint bioluminescence of the deep, shimmering with the colors of a fresh bruise, violent violets, necrotic blacks, and the deep, oxygen-starved blue of suffocated blood. It possesses the head of a horse, but a horse that has drowned a thousand times, its mane a tangle of swaying kelp and stinging anemones, its eyes wide, white, and sightless, staring into a dimension that existed before light. The tail is a vast fan of translucent fin that ripples with enough force to generate tsunamis. It is not just an animal. It is the embodiment of the chaotic, devouring energy of the sea, the hunger that seeks to dissolve the hard edges of the land back into the soup of the primeval. It is the force that does not want to rule the world. It wants to swallow it.

Kai Kai wakes up. The slumber is broken not by a thought, but by an irritation. It feels the world above. It feels the dryness of the land pressing down on the water like a heavy lid. It tastes the stagnation in the currents. The humans have stopped singing to the water. They have stopped fearing the deep. They are walking on the earth as if it belongs to them. This makes the water heavy. Kai Kai does not think in complex sentences. It thinks in urges. It thinks in pressure. "Too still," the serpent feels. "Too hard. Too dry. The land is stiff. I hate the stiff. I want soft. I want wet. I want all." The desire rises like a poisonous bubble from the muck. It is not a plan. It is a hunger. "Break it," the urge whispers. "Wet it. Make it mine. Time for soup."

It begins with a sound. Not a roar, but a hiss. A low, sibilant whisper that rises from the surf. "Kai... Kai... Kai..." It is a hypnotic rhythm, syncing with the pulse of the blood. The infiltration of the village begins not with water, but with dreams. At night, the people toss on their mats, their minds invaded by a damp, pressurized dread. They dream of drowning, but not in clean ocean water. They dream of a viscous, oily fluid that smells of things that have been dead for a thousand years. They feel their lungs filling not with air, but with a cold, heavy silence. In these dreams, the geometry of their homes is wrong; the angles are soft, wet, and pulsating. They see the familiar faces of their loved ones, but the eyes are wide and lidless, staring with the blank indifference of fish. They wake up gasping, their sheets soaked with a sweat that tastes of brine, their hearts hammering against their ribs. Yet, even as they wake, the sound does not stop. It is a subsonic vibration that rattles the bones of the skull. It is coming from the beach.

The water begins to rise. It does not rise like a normal tide, predictable and governed by the moon. It rises with a dark, sentient intent. The waves do not crash; they surge. They do not break; they invade. They slide up the sand like wet, grasping fingers, cold and relentless, clutching at the dunes, pulling the dry land back into the foaming surf. The rivers, sensing the call of their master, stop their flow. They turn back on themselves. They begin to flow backward, upstream, carrying the salt into the heart of the sweet valleys. The lakes swell, bursting their banks with a sudden, violent expansion. Above, the sky mirrors the ocean below. It turns a bruised, swollen purple, heavy with clouds that look like lesions on the face of the heavens. The rain begins. It is not a nourishing rain that feeds the crops. It is a deluge. It is a wall of gray water falling from the sky, a vertical ocean that dissolves the mud bricks of the houses into sludge, extinguishing the sacred fires of the hearths with a final, hissing gasp.

Panic seizes the people, a cold fluid terror that floods the mind. They watch as the order of their lives is simply washed away. The fences they built to divide "mine" from "yours," the boundaries they thought were real, are gone in an instant, submerged beneath a uniform, indifferent gray sheet. The roads are gone. The landmarks are gone. The definitions of the world are being erased by the universal solvent of the flood. There is no more geometry. There is no more history. There is only the rising level, the wet erasure of everything that was once solid.

Kai Kai Vilu rises from the waves. Its massive head towers over the coastline. It screams, a sound like a tearing sheet of metal. It commands the waters to take everything. It wants to return the cosmos to the watery womb of non-existence. It wants to drown the ego of the world.

The people run. They run toward the only thing that remains solid. The mountains.

But the mountains are not dead rock. They are the carapace of a living will. They are the body of the other serpent, **Tren Tren Vilu***, the Serpent of the Earth. If Kai Kai is the chaotic fluid, Tren Tren is the rigid spine of structure, the force of elevation, the vertical imperative to survive. It sleeps in the granite roots of the Andes. It feels the scream of Kai Kai vibrating through the bedrock. It feels the cold, biting insult of the rising salt water lapping against its flanks, threatening to dissolve the integrity of the land. And so, it wakes up.*

Tren Tren cries out. Its voice is not a hiss; it is the rumble of a tectonic plate shifting. "Tren... Tren... Tren..." It is a sound of warning that bypasses the ears and shakes the teeth in the skull. It is a frequency of pure urgency. It calls to the people not with love, but with the desperate command of a parent seeing a child in front of a train. "Come up," the earth screams. "Come up or die." The ground shudders underfoot, no longer a passive stage, but a moving elevator pushing toward the sky.

The people scramble up the slopes, but it is not a climb. It is a desperate clawing against the earth. Mud, thick and treacherous, slicks their feet, turning the solid ground into a sliding trap that wants to pull them back down. They carry nothing but their children on their backs, the warm weight of the future clinging to their necks. Behind them, the trail is littered with the debris of a former life. Tools, gold, heavy woven cloaks. All dropped. All abandoned. The flood demands a total stripping of the self. It demands poverty. You cannot swim with gold in your pockets, and you cannot climb with the weight of who you used to be.

But the water is faster. It does not move with the clumsiness of a wave. It rises with the smooth, terrifying speed of a filling lung. Kai Kai Vilu is relentless. The ocean swells higher, a dark, liquid wall chasing them up the slopes, lapping at their heels with a cold, predatory intimacy. They look back, and the world is gone. The valleys where they loved are gone. The foothills where they hunted are gone. Swallowed whole by the indifference of the deep. Only the peaks remain now. Tiny, fragile islands of life shrinking by the second in a rising sea of death.

Tren Tren fights back. It does not fight with claws. It fights with elevation. As the water rises, the mountain rises. The earth arches its back. It pushes itself upward, straining against gravity, growing taller by the second to keep its children above the foam. It is a race between the fluid chaos and the solid will.

The people are terrified. The air grows thin. The sun burns them from above, while the water freezes them from below. They are trapped in the liminal zone between the scorching sky and the drowning deep. They crowd onto the peaks, shoulder to shoulder, no longer rich or poor, no longer enemies or friends. They are just meat trying not to drown.

But the water keeps rising. Kai Kai is powerful. It covers the lower peaks, swallowing the earth one stone at a time. Those who are too slow, those who are weighed down by fear or age or the heavy gold of their past lives, are overtaken. And here, the magic of Neptune reveals its double edge. The flood does not just kill. It transforms. It does not offer the finality of death but the mutation of life.

As the water swallows the people, they do not simply die. They change. They feel the cold salt stinging their eyes, but then the sting fades into a strange, numbing comfort. Their skin turns silvery and scaly, shedding the soft vulnerability of the mammal for the armored sleekness of the fish. Their legs, once useful for climbing mountains, become useless drag. They fuse together, knitting bone to bone and flesh to flesh until they form a single, muscular tail that thrashes against the current. Their lungs shift. The burning need for air vanishes, replaced by the cool intake of oxygenated water through slits that open in their necks. They become fish. They become dolphins (shumpall). They become cetaceans.

They are saved, but they are no longer human. They have regressed. They have returned to the unconscious, slipping back down the evolutionary ladder to a place where there is no "I" and no "you." They swim away into the dark, forgetting their names. They forget the language of their fathers. They forget the fire and the mountain. They dissolve into the bliss of the school, moving as one vast, shimmering mind through the silence of the deep.

This is the danger of the flood. It offers a solution to suffering. It offers the end of the struggle. Just let go. Just sink. Become a fish. Forget the pain of being a man.

Those who remain on the peaks of Tren Tren fight the seduction. They cling to the rock. They protect their heads from the sun with clay pots, which fuse to their skulls, marking them forever. They witness the world ending. They see the familiar landscape erased, turned into a mirror of the sky.

The battle lasts for aeons, or perhaps only for a night. Time dissolves in the flood. Finally, a balance is reached. Tren Tren rises so high that it touches the sun. Kai Kai can push the water no higher without dissolving itself. The two serpents stare at each other across the waterline. The fluid and the solid. The unconscious and the ego. They hiss. They lock into a stalemate. A truce is formed. The water recedes, but not all the way. The geography is changed forever. New islands are formed. New bays are carved. The world is not what it was.

The survivors begin the slow descent. The mud is drying now, cracking into gray scales under the returning sun. They move tentatively, their legs heavy with the memory of the climb. They are few. They are changed. The silence of the mountain still rings in their ears, a stark contrast to the roar that swallowed their previous lives. As they reach the lower slopes, they do not find their old valleys. They find a new geography. The coastline has been redrawn by the violence of the water. New bays carve into the land where forests once stood. Salt dries white on the rocks, a crystalline memory of the invasion.

They step onto the flat land, but it feels different beneath their feet. It feels provisional. They look at the dry earth not as a given, but as a temporary truce. They build new fires, but they watch the smoke rise with a different kind of attention. They know now that the solid world is a thin crust floating over a depth that has no bottom. They know that beneath the surface of the real, beneath the mundane tasks of gathering wood and cooking food, the great serpent is always waiting. It sleeps with one eye open, its coils shifting in the dark, ready to rise again when the memory of the water fades.

III. The Reflection

The myth of the Great Flood is universal, but the Mapuche version offers a specific, haunting insight into the **Neptunian** experience. Unlike the Biblical flood, which is a moral punishment from a distant God, the war between Kai Kai and Tren Tren is a psychological structural reality. It is the eternal tension between the **Oceanic Unconscious** and the **Elevating Ego**.

The Oceanic Feeling and the ***Objet petit a***

Sigmund Freud, in his correspondence with Romain Rolland, famously discussed the "Oceanic Feeling": a sensation of eternity, a feeling as of something limitless, unbounded, as it were, "oceanic" (Freud 1930). Kai Kai Vilu is the embodiment of this feeling in its threatening aspect. Neptune represents the urge to dissolve. We all carry a secret exhaustion. The burden of being an individual, of having a name, a job, a history, a separation from others, is heavy. Saturn weighs us down. Neptune whispers a seductive promise: "Put down the weight. Dissolve. Return to the water."

However, this return is not merely a regression; it is a structural attempt to solve the riddle of desire. As posited in recent research on Neptune and the object-cause of desire, the return to the womb (or the ocean) is an impossible but seductive strategy for attaining the **objet petit a**. This object, the cause of our desire, is the remnant of the Real that we lost when we entered language. By dissolving the subject into the oceanic mass, the addict or mystic hopes to merge with the object-cause itself, thereby ending the lack that defines human existence (Meza 2025). The transformation of the people into fish is the perfect metaphor for this. To become a fish is to attain the object by sacrificing the subject. They are "saved" from the pain of lack but lost to the world of meaning (Jung 1959).

The Inflation of the Ego: Tren Tren

If Kai Kai is the threat of psychosis or addiction (being swallowed), Tren Tren represents the defense mechanism against it. Notice how Tren Tren fights. It *rises*. It grows taller. In clinical terms, when the unconscious threatens to flood the psyche (depression, overwhelming emotion), the ego often reacts with **Inflation** or Mania. We get "high." We scramble up the mountain. We adopt a position of grandiosity or spiritual superiority to stay above the water. This is the "High Ground" of the neurotic. "I am not sad; I am enlightened." "I am not lonely; I am solitary." The danger of Tren Tren is that it can lift us so high that we burn in the sun (as the myth details). We become disconnected from the earth, scorched by the solar fire of the intellect or spirit, just to avoid getting wet. A healthy psyche is not one that lives permanently on the peak of Tren Tren, nor one that swims forever with Kai Kai. It is the psyche that lives in the valleys after the water has receded, respecting both the height and the depth.

The Lacanian Real and the Fluidity of Meaning

From a Lacanian perspective, the flood represents the invasion of the **Real**. The Symbolic Order (civilization, language, the "fences" and "roads" mentioned in the myth) is built on dry land. It relies on distinctions. "This is not that." Water erases distinctions. The flood is the collapse of the Symbolic. Meaning becomes fluid. Categories dissolve. This is the experience of the psychotic break or the mystic rapture (Lacan 1976). The "Name-of-the-Father" (which separates and orders) is drowned by the voice of the Serpent. However, this dissolution is also the source of all creativity. The flood rearranges the world. The old, rigid structures (the "Golden Age" of Saturn from the previous chapter) are washed away. Neptune creates new islands. It creates new coastlines. The artist, the poet, and the healer must dip into the waters of Kai

Kai to retrieve the new forms, but they must have the strength of Tren Tren to bring them back to dry land without drowning.

The Pharmakon: Poison and Cure

The Greeks had a word, *Pharmakon*, which meant both "poison" and "cure." Neptune is the ultimate Pharmakon. The water that drowns is also the water that cleanses. The drug that kills is also the medicine that numbs the unbearable pain. The myth ends with a standoff, a balance. This is the wisdom of Neptune. We cannot "kill" the unconscious (Kai Kai cannot be slain). We can only learn to live in dynamic relationship with it. We must know where the high ground is (our spiritual practice, our discipline, our support network) so that when the waters rise, we have a place to stand. But we must also honor the water, for a world without Kai Kai is a desert.

Integration Practice: The High Ground

Ask yourself: Where is the water rising in your life?

- **Identify the Flood:** Look for areas where you feel overwhelmed, where boundaries are blurring, or where you are checking out. Are you numbing yourself with food, substances, or distraction? Are you feeling a "flooding" of emotion that makes it hard to function? This is the hiss of Kai Kai.

- **Locate the Mountain:** What is your Tren Tren? What is the solid ground you can stand on when the emotions rise? It might be a routine. It might be a physical space (a gym, a church, a garden). It might be a relationship that holds you accountable.

- **The Sun Hat:** In the myth, the survivors wore clay pots to protect themselves from the sun. This symbolizes protecting your mind while you are in a survival state. Do not try to "figure it out" when you are drowning. Just get to high ground. Protect your head.

Practice: Create a "Flood Protocol." When you feel the urge to numb out or the panic of overwhelm, write down three physical steps to take you to high ground. Example: 1. Put phone in drawer. 2. Drink a glass of cold water. 3. Walk outside and touch a tree. Move from the fluid to the solid.

IV. References

- **Bacigalupo, A. M.** (2007). *Shamans of the Foye Tree: Gender, Power, and Healing among the Chilean Mapuche.* Austin: University of Texas Press.

- **Cooper, J. M.** (1946). The Araucanians. In *Handbook of South American Indians, Vol. 2.* Washington: Government Printing Office.

- **Faron, L. C.** (1964). *Hawks of the Sun: Mapuche Morality and Its Ritual Attributes.* Pittsburgh: University of Pittsburgh Press.

- **Freud, S.** (1930). *Civilization and Its Discontents.* (J. Strachey, Trans.). London: The Hogarth Press.

- **Greene, L.** (1996). *The Astrological Neptune and the Quest for Redemption.* York Beach, ME: Samuel Weiser.

- **Jung, C. G.** (1959). *The Archetypes and the Collective Unconscious* (Collected Works of C.G. Jung, Vol. 9, Part 1). Princeton: Princeton University Press.

- **Lacan, J.** (1976). *The Seminar of Jacques Lacan, Book XXIII: The Sinthome.* (A.R. Price, Trans.). Cambridge: Polity Press.

- **Meza, G.** (2025). *Neptune and the Object-Cause of Desire.* Retrieved from https://www.astro-rose.fr/en/journal

10 PLUTO: DEATH AND REBIRTH

Archetype: Transformation, Power, The Shadow, The Hidden Treasure
Myth: Inanna's Descent into the Underworld (Sumerian)

I. The Context: The Wealth of the Deep

We have reached the edge of the known system. Beyond the dissolution of Neptune lies the small, cold, rocky body that governs the most terrifying and necessary process of the human experience. Pluto.

In Roman mythology, Pluto is the Lord of the Underworld, but his name comes from the Greek *Plouton*, meaning "The Wealthy One." This linguistic connection reveals a profound psychological truth. The gold, the diamonds, the oil, the roots of the trees, all the hidden riches of the earth are located in the domain of death. To find the treasure, one must descend.

Pluto represents the principle of **Metamorphosis**. Unlike the swift changes of Mercury or the expansion of Jupiter, Plutonic change is nuclear. It is the total destruction of the old form to release the energy trapped within it. It is the caterpillar dissolving into soup within the chrysalis. It is the forest fire that clears the deadwood so that the seeds of the sequoia can crack open.

To explore this archetype, we journey back to the very dawn of written history, to ancient Sumer. We look to the first great epic of the descent, recorded on clay tablets over 4,000 years ago: **The Descent of Inanna** (Wolkstein & Kramer 1983). It is the story of the Queen of Heaven, articulated beautifully by the high priestess Enheduanna (Meador 2000), who voluntarily strips herself of every power, every title, and every protection to confront her dark sister in the Great Below. It teaches us that true power is not found in accumulation, but in the radical courage to let everything go.

II. The Myth

I invite you to find a posture of absolute grounding. Feel the floor beneath your feet, not just as a surface, but as the roof of something else. Visualize the layers of soil, rock, water, and magma that stretch for thousands of miles beneath your chair. You are sitting on top of a great depth. Let your breath drop all the way down to the base of your spine. Let your gaze soften and your focus turn inward, dimming the light of the upper world. You are entering the realm of the Great Below.

Imagine a sky of blinding white heat. It is the sky of ancient Sumer, hanging over the fertile crescent like a hammer of hammered bronze. The light here is not gentle. It is absolute. It bleaches the color from the reeds and turns the mud of the riverbanks into hard, cracked pavement. You are walking through the streets of Uruk, the first true city of mankind. Feel the dust coating your skin, a fine, gritty powder that tastes of ancient clay. The air is thick, almost solid with the noise of civilization being born. It is a cacophony of life. You hear the bleating of goats being driven to market, the rhythmic thud of the potter's wheel, the sharp cries of merchants selling barley, onions, and beer. It smells of unwashed bodies sweating in the sun, of roasting meat turning on spits, of the sweet, rotting vegetation of the Euphrates, and the sharp, acrid smoke of burning dung.

Push through the crowd. Move past the scribes pressing their reed styluses into wet tablets, recording the inventory of the world. Move past the soldiers with their copper spears. Look up. Rising above the chaos of the streets, dominating the horizon, are the walls of the sacred precinct. The Eanna District. And rising from within those walls is the Ziggurat. It is a mountain built by human hands, a stairway of mud-brick rising terrace upon terrace toward the heavens. It is painted in colors that shock the eye against the beige of the desert. White, black, and red. At the very top, shimmering in the heat haze, is the temple itself. It is the house of the god, the place where the vertical power of the sky touches the horizontal plane of the earth.

On the highest terrace stands Inanna. She is a vision of terrifying perfection, a being who seems to absorb the sunlight and radiate it back with double the intensity. Her skin glows with the sheen of scented oil, dark and luminous like polished copper. Her eyes are large, rimmed with heavy black kohl, staring out over her dominion with an gaze that is both erotic and imperious. She is dressed in the full regalia of her station. Upon her head rests the Shugurra, the crown of the steppe, a heavy golden band that marks her as the supreme consciousness. Strands of lapis lazuli, blue as the deep night sky, are draped around her neck, cooling the heat of her skin. A breastplate of gold covers her chest, inscribed with the words "Come, Man, Come," a declaration of her power to attract and consume. Her royal robe, dyed in the rich purples and reds of sovereignty, falls to her feet in heavy folds that do not stir in the wind. She holds the rod and the line of measurement, the tools of the architect, the symbols that she defines the boundaries of reality. Her aura is not soft. It is a hum of high-voltage power, the vibration of a goddess who encompasses both the fertility of the field and the slaughter of the battlefield. She is the Queen of Heaven and Earth. She has everything. She has the temples. She has the love of the people. She has the crops that grow tall in the mud of the Euphrates. She is the goddess of the morning star and the evening star, the lady of sexual love and the lady of war. She is the ego at the height of its power and integration.

But then, a sound intrudes upon the perfection. It does not come from the sky, where the birds sing. It comes from beneath the floor. It is a vibration that travels up through the soles of her feet, a tremor that shakes the golden dust motes in the air. Inanna kneels. She presses her ear against the baked clay bricks of her palace floor, listening to the foundation of her world. Perhaps you can hear it too, or do you just feel it in your bones?

The sound becomes a groan. It is not a human sound. It is a low, guttural cry that seems to originate from the tectonic plates of the psyche. It is the sound of pain that has been buried alive. It smells of old earth, of dry rot, of blood that has turned to black powder. It is a cry of raw, unmetabolized instinct that has been denied the light of the sun.

It is the voice of her older sister, Ereshkigal, the Queen of the Great Below. Ereshkigal is the dark mirror of Inanna. While Inanna receives the golden wheat and the worship of the living, Ereshkigal receives the dry dust and the silence of the dead. She is the widow who mourns in the dark. She is the mother who has lost her children to the void. She is the rage of everything that has been repressed, forgotten, and shoved underground to keep the surface beautiful.

Inanna knows that her reign is incomplete. She has the light, but she does not have the depth. She calls to her faithful servant, Ninshubur. "I am going down," she says. Her voice is calm, but it carries the weight of a final testament. "I am going to the 'Land of No Return.' If I do not come back in three days, you must mourn for me. You must beat the drum in the assembly. You must beg the fathers, Enlil, Nanna, and Enki, to save me. Do not let me die in the dark."

Inanna prepares. She does not dress for a funeral. She dresses for a coronation. She gathers the ***Me****, the seven divine powers of civilization, wrapping them around her body like armor. She places the Shugurra, the crown of the steppe, upon her head. It is not a delicate tiara. It is a heavy, golden band that presses against her temples, signifying the weight of the horizon itself. She arranges the dark locks of hair across her forehead with deliberate care, framing her face to be seen, to be witnessed. She takes the small lapis lazuli beads, cold and smooth as river stones, and ties them around her neck. They rest against the hollow of her throat, the seat of her voice and her command. She lets the double strand of beads fall to her breast. They are heavy, clicking softly against her skin, a physical reminder of her heart's value. She covers her body with the royal robe of the Pala. It is dyed the deep, imperial purple of the twilight sky, woven from the finest wool, draping her form in the authority of the queenship. She dips her finger into the jar of kohl. She paints her eyes with the ointment called "Let him come, let him come." It is a black, smoky line that sharpens her gaze into a weapon of seduction. She places the pectoral of chaotic brilliance on her chest. It catches the light, flashing with a dangerous, unpredictable fire. She slips the gold ring onto her wrist, the cold metal circling the pulse of her life. Finally, she takes the lapis lazuli measuring rod and line in her hand. These* *are not weapons of war. They are the tools of the architect, the symbols that she alone defines the boundaries of reality.*

She is armored in her identity. She is armored in her status. She walks to the gate of the underworld, the Ganzir, the place where the dry dust begins.

She knocks. The sound echoes in the cavernous silence. "Open the gate, Neti!" she cries. "I am Inanna, Queen of Heaven, on my way to the East."

Neti, the chief gatekeeper of the underworld, looks through the slit. He sees the radiant goddess. He sees the power. But he does not open the gate. The laws of the underworld are not the laws of the upper world. He goes to Ereshkigal. "My queen," he says. "Inanna is at the gate. She is dressed in all her powers."

Ereshkigal bites her thigh in anger. She knows why Inanna has come. The light wants to colonize the dark. "Let her in," Ereshkigal says, her voice like grinding stones. "But follow the ancient rites. At each of the seven gates, strip her of one of her powers. Let her enter naked and bowed low."

Neti returns. The heavy bolt slides back. The first gate opens.

Inanna steps through. The air is stale and cold. Neti reaches out. "My Lady," he says. "Give me the ***Crown of the Steppe****." "Why?" Inanna asks. "This is my crown. It signifies my sovereignty. It signifies that I am the head, the ruler, the one who thinks and decides." "Quiet, Inanna," Neti replies. "The ways of the underworld are perfect. They may not be questioned." Inanna hesitates. She feels the metal circle lift from her head. Without it, she feels lighter, but also smaller. Her thoughts, usually so sharp and commanding, feel suddenly exposed to the cold air. She walks on.*

At the second gate, Neti stops her again. He holds out his hand. "My Lady," he says. "Give me the ***Wig of hair****." "Why?" Inanna asks. "This is my beauty. It signifies my allure, the way I frame my face for the world to see." "Quiet, Inanna," Neti replies. "The ways of the underworld are perfect. They may not be questioned." Inanna touches her forehead. She unpins the dark locks. Her face is now bare, stripped of the frame. She feels plain. She feels ordinary.*

At the third gate, Neti blocks the path. "My Lady," he says. "Give me the ***Lapis Lazuli Beads*** *around your neck." "Why?" Inanna asks. "These are the beads of the throat. They signify my voice, my ability to speak, to command, to sing." "Quiet, Inanna," Neti replies. "The ways of the underworld are perfect. They may not be questioned." As Neti unclasps them, she feels a silence rising in her throat. Her words no longer carry the weight of authority. She is losing the power of communication.*

At the fourth gate, Neti points to her chest. "My Lady," he says. "Give me the ***Double Strand of Beads*** *on your breast." "Why?" Inanna asks. "These protect my heart. They signify my emotions, my loves, my attachments." "Quiet, Inanna," Neti replies. "The ways* *of the underworld are perfect. They may not be questioned." Inanna hands them over. Her chest feels cold. Her heart is no longer shielded by her relationships or her lovers. She is becoming vulnerable.*

At the fifth gate, Neti reaches for her hand. "My Lady," he says. "Give me the **Gold Ring** *from your wrist." "Why?" Inanna asks. "This is my commitment. It signifies my agency, the hand that grasps, the hand that marries, the hand that signs contracts." "Quiet, Inanna," Neti replies. "The ways of the underworld are perfect. They may not be questioned." Without it, she has no legal standing. She is no longer a wife or a ruler. She is just a woman with empty hands.*

At the sixth gate, Neti looks at her armor. "My Lady," he says. "Give me the **Breastplate** *called 'Come, Man, Come'." "Why?" Inanna asks. "This is my sexual power. It signifies my identity as a desirable object." "Quiet, Inanna," Neti replies. "The ways of the underworld are perfect. They may not be questioned." Neti unbuckles it. It falls to the dusty floor with a dull thud. She is no longer the object of desire. She is just flesh.*

Finally, at the seventh gate, the last barrier between the ego and the abyss, Neti demands everything that is left. "My Lady," he says. "Give me the **Royal Robe** *and the* **Measuring Rod***." "Why?" Inanna asks. "This is my dignity and my intellect. They signify my ability to judge, to measure, to define boundaries." "Quiet, Inanna," Neti replies. "The ways of the underworld are perfect. They may not be questioned." Inanna stands trembling. She is stripped of everything. Her mind, her beauty, her voice, her heart, her agency, her sexuality, and finally, her judgment. She is naked.*

"Enter," Neti says.

She steps across the threshold into the throne room of Ereshkigal. Notice how the air changes here. It becomes thick, almost liquid, sticking to the skin like a cold sweat. This is not a place of glory. It is a damp, rotting cave, the hollowed-out womb of the earth where all things eventually return. You can smell it. It is the scent of wet clay, of stagnant water, of flowers that have been left too long on a grave. The walls weep with moisture, slick and dark, reflecting no light.

In the center of this shadow sits the Queen. Ereshkigal. She sits on a throne not of gold, but of bone, the white, calcified remains of those who have come before. Look at her. She is not beautiful in the way of the upper world. Her hair is a tangled mass, matted with the gray dirt of the grave, heavy and unwashed. Her body is naked and swollen, distended not with food, but with the grief of a thousand funerals. She holds the weight of every tear ever shed. She is raw. She is the color of bruises and earth. Around her stand the Anunna, the seven judges of the dead. They are silent, immobile figures carved from living rock. Their eyes fix on the intruder with a judgment that is beyond morality. They are simply the witnesses of the inevitable.

Inanna, the Great Queen, is brought low. She kneels in the dust. She looks up at her sister. She expects a reunion. She expects understanding.

But Ereshkigal fixes her with the **Eye of Death**. *It is a gaze that contains no reflection. It is the gaze of the biological reality that does not care about your titles. Then the Anunna, the seven judges, rise from the shadows. They surround her. They pass judgment against her.*

They unleash the attack. It is not physical, yet it tears the soul. They look at her, it is the look of death. They speak to her, it is the speech of anger. They shout at her, it is the shout of heavy guilt. The sound is a physical force, a sonic weapon that batters the naked goddess. Ereshkigal strikes. She strikes her sister. The afflicted woman is turned into a corpse. The flesh turns green. The warmth leaves the blood. She becomes a piece of rotting meat. And she is hung on a hook on the wall.

Imagine that image. The Queen of Heaven, who ruled the world, is now a slab of meat hanging in the dark. She has no consciousness. She has no future. She has ceased to exist as a subject. She is pure object. She is dead.

Three days pass. In the upper world, a terrifying silence descends. It is not the quiet of rest; it is the quiet of a stopped heart. Nature does not just pause; it ceases. The great engines of biology, usually so noisy with desire and growth, grind to a halt. In the fields, the bulls stand like statues of clay, their eyes dull and heavy, looking at the cows with a profound, unnatural indifference. The urge to merge, to create, to continue the line, has simply evaporated. In the cities, the men turn away from the women, and the women turn away from the men. The beds are cold. The touch of skin on skin elicits no spark, no warmth, only the dry friction of dead leaves rubbing together. The libido of the world has gone underground.

The grain does not sprout. The seeds lie in the furrows, dormant and refusing to wake. They sense that the animating spirit is gone. The sap stops flowing in the trees, leaving the leaves brittle and gray. The rivers seem to flow slower, thick with silt. Without the feminine principle of life, the world is drained of color. It becomes a desert of gray dust, a monochrome wasteland where time continues to pass, but nothing happens. It is a world without future, a flat, endless present of stagnation.

Ninshubur, the faithful servant, keeps the promise. She does not let the silence of the world stop her. She beats the drum of mourning in the assembly, a slow, hollow rhythm that mimics a dying heart. She tears her eyes. She tears her mouth. She circles the temples of the great gods, begging for intervention.

She goes first to Enlil, the god of air, in his great temple at Nippur. She falls to her knees on the cold stone. "Father Enlil," she cries. "Do not let your daughter be put to death in the underworld. Do not let your good metal be covered with the dust of the grave. Do not let your precious lapis lazuli be broken into the stone of the mason."

But Enlil sits high on his throne of wind. He looks down at her with eyes that are as distant and cold as the stratosphere. He is the keeper of the tablets of destiny, the god of separation. To him, Inanna's descent is not a tragedy; it is a transgression. "She craved the Great Below," he says, his voice stripping the hope from the air. "She who has all the powers of the sky wanted the powers of the earth as well. She violated the boundaries. The laws of the cosmos are clear. Those who go down do not come up. Let her stay where she chose to go."

Ninshubur travels on. She goes to Ur, to the temple of Nanna, the moon god. "Father Nanna," she pleads. "Do not let your daughter be killed. Do not let the wood of the boxwood tree be cut into splinters."

Nanna looks at her. His face is pale, changing, reflecting only the light of others, offering no warmth of his own. He is the father who fears the ambition of the child. "She asked for too much," he whispers, a dry, dusty sound. "She held the Me of the heavens, and yet she hungered for the Me of the depths. Such hunger is dangerous. It disrupts the balance. If she has been judged by the Seven Judges, then she is guilty. I will not interfere."

But Enki, the god of wisdom and water, the god of the depths, listens. He grieves. He understands that the world cannot survive without Inanna, but he also knows she cannot return as she was. He reaches under his fingernail and pulls out some dirt. From this humble filth, he shapes two strange creatures: the ***Kurgarra*** *and the* ***Galatur****. They are neither male nor female. They are sexless, liminal beings who can slip through the cracks of the gates unnoticed. They are like flies.*

Enki gives them the food of life and the water of life. He gives them a specific instruction. "Do not fight Ereshkigal," he says. "Do not try to be strong. Listen to her. When she groans, you groan."

The creatures fly down. They slip past the seven gates. They enter the throne room. Ereshkigal is in agony. She is lying on the ground, moaning with the pain of a birth that cannot happen, the pain of endless death. "Oh, my inside," she groans. "Oh, your inside," the Kurgarra echoes softly. "Oh, my outside," she cries. "Oh, your outside," the Galatur whispers.

Ereshkigal stops. She looks at them. For the first time in eternity, someone has heard her. Someone has mirrored her pain without trying to fix it or judge it. "Who are you?" she asks. "If you are gods, I will bless you. If you are mortals, I will give you a gift."

They ask for only one thing. "Give us the corpse that hangs on the hook."

Ereshkigal gestures to the wall with a hand heavy with boredom. To her, the body is nothing more than refuse. It is a discarded husk that clutters her domain. She allows them to take it, indifferent to its value, for in the underworld, all flesh is merely waiting to be dust. The Kurgarra and the Galatur approach the hook with reverence. They do not touch the goddess with their hands. They use the instruments of grace. They take the pouch given by Enki. They take the flask. With trembling precision, they sprinkle the ***Water of Life*** *upon the gray, cold skin. It hisses as it touches the death-pallor, sinking into the pores like rain into a desert. They crumble the* ***Food of Life*** *onto her lips, forcing the first grain of sustenance past the barrier of her teeth.*

Then, the miracle occurs. A shudder runs through the meat. It is violent. It is a galvanic shock that convulses the muscles. The green tint of decay fades, replaced by the flush of blood remembering its course. Inanna gasps. It is a terrible sound. It is the sound of air rushing into a vacuum, the scream of the lungs expanding against the weight of the earth. The eye opens. It is not the eye of the Queen who descended. It is an eye that has seen the bottom. She pulls herself from the hook, sliding down the wall to collapse on the dusty floor. She is heaving. She is alive. But she is forever marked by the iron that held her.

She is alive. But she is not the same. She has the smell of the grave on her skin. She has the knowledge of the hook in her bones. She begins the ascent.

She approaches the first gate of the return, which was the last gate of her sorrow. Neti is waiting. "My Lady," he says. "Take back the ***Royal Robe*** *and the* ***Measuring Rod****." Inanna takes the tools of the intellect and the dignity of her body. She wraps the purple wool around her shoulders. She holds the rod. But the weight is different. Before, they were her authority. Now, they are tools. She knows she is the one who holds them, not the one defined by them. She walks on.*

At the next gate, Neti holds out the golden armor. "My Lady," he says. "Take back the ***Breastplate*** *called 'Come, Man, Come'." Inanna buckles the gold over her chest. The seduction returns, the allure returns, but she feels the cold metal against skin that has known the chill of the meat hook. She knows her value is not in the gold, but in the heart beating beneath it.*

At the third gate of the ascent, Neti offers the circle of gold. "My Lady," he says. "Take back the ***Gold Ring****." She slips it onto her wrist. The symbol of commitment and agency. But she remembers the empty hands that hung in the dark. She knows that even without the ring, she exists.*

At the fourth gate, Neti presents the gems. "My Lady," he says. "Take back the ***Double Strand of Beads****." She clasps them over her breast. The emotions, the loves, the attachments. They settle against her skin, but they no longer shield her heart. Her heart is open, broken by death and healed by grace, too vast to be contained by a string of stones.*

At the fifth gate, Neti holds out the blue stones. "My Lady," he says. "Take back the ***Lapis Lazuli Beads****." She ties them around her neck. Her voice returns. Her command returns. But the silence of the underworld is still underneath her tongue. She will speak, but she will never again speak with the arrogance of one who has not screamed in the dark.*

At the sixth gate, Neti offers the frame of beauty. "My Lady," he says. "Take back the ***Wig of hair****." Inanna places the dark locks upon her head. The persona is restored. The frame is back. But she looks out from under the hair with eyes that have seen the Eye of Death. She knows the face is just a mask.*

Finally, at the last gate, the threshold of the upper world, Neti holds the heavy band of gold. "My Lady," he says. "Take back the ***Crown of the Steppe****." Inanna places the crown upon her head. The sovereignty returns. The ego is reinstated. She stands in the full regalia of the Queen of Heaven. To the observer, she looks exactly as she did when she left. But she knows the truth. She feels the heavy garments resting on a body that was, only moments ago, a corpse. She wears them, but she knows she is not them. She knows that underneath the gold, she is meat.*

She emerges into the sunlight. But the law of the underworld is strict: a head for a head. If she returns, someone must take her place. The Galla, the demons of the underworld, cling to her side. They are hungry. They want a substitute.

Inanna walks through her cities. She sees her servant Ninshubur dressed in rags, mourning in the dust. "Take her," the demons say. "No," Inanna says. "She fought for me." She sees her son, Shara, dressed in haircloth, weeping. "Take him," the demons say. "No," Inanna says. "He mourned for me."

Then she comes to the great apple tree in Uruk. There, sitting on her throne, dressed in shining garments, is her husband, ***Dumuzi****. He is not mourning. He is enjoying his power. He has not missed her. He is wearing her robe. He is eating her food.*

Inanna looks at him with the Eye of Death she learned from Ereshkigal. She realizes that while she was undergoing the transformation of the tomb, he remained in the stagnation of the ego. He has not grown. He has merely occupied the space she left.

"Take him," she whispers.

The demons seize Dumuzi. He is dragged down to the Great Below to pay the price of consciousness. Inanna stands alone under the apple tree. She has lost her husband, but she has gained her soul. She has united the height of heaven with the depth of hell. She is whole.

III. The Reflection

The myth of Inanna is the master blueprint for the process of **Plutonic Transformation**. Unlike the hero myths where the protagonist slays a monster, this is a myth of **Subjective Destitution**. The hero does not conquer; the hero is dismantled (Campbell 1949).

The Descent and the Stripping of the Persona

The journey through the seven gates is a precise map of what happens during a Plutonic transit or a "Dark Night of the Soul." Pluto demands the surrender of the **Persona** (the social mask). When we face a crisis, be it a divorce, a bankruptcy, a terminal diagnosis or a deep depression, we often feel that we are being stripped.

- The "Crown" (our professional status) is taken.
- The "Ring" (our agency/marriage) is taken.
- The "Voice" (our ability to explain ourselves) is taken.

We protest, like Inanna, crying out "But this is mine! This is who I am!" And the answer of the Underworld is always the same: "Quiet. The ways of the underworld are perfect." We must understand that this stripping is not a punishment. It is a necessity. The ego structures (the garments) have become too small, too rigid, or too false to contain the growth of the Self. We cannot be reborn if we are still wearing the clothes of the past. We must become naked to be renewed (Brinton Perera 1981).

As James Hollis argues, these "swamplands of the soul" (guilt, grief, loneliness, anxiety) are not pathologies to be cured, but meaningful tasks to be lived. They are dismal places, yes, but they are also the only places where the new life can be forged. The soul does not grow in the bright sunshine of the ego's certainty. It grows in the dark, wet soil of the descent. To bypass the swamp is to bypass the soul itself (Hollis 1996).

The Meat on the Hook: Subjective Destitution

The most terrifying image in the myth is Inanna hanging as a corpse on a hook. In Lacanian psychoanalysis, this corresponds to the concept of **Subjective Destitution**. This is the moment at the end of analysis (or at the bottom of a crisis) where the subject realizes that all their identifications ("I am a mother," "I am a CEO," "I am a good person") are empty signifiers. When Inanna is on the hook, she is no longer "The Queen." She is just biological matter. She confronts the **Real** of her own mortality. She confronts the absolute zero of existence. Derek Hook describes this not merely as a loss, but as a radical 'evacuation' of the imaginary identifications that shore up the ego. It is a reduction to the absolute zero of the subject, where one is no longer sustained by the desire of the Other (Hook 2017).

This is the state of the *Nigredo* in alchemy, but deepened. It is not just blackness; it is rot. It is the realization that the Ego is not the master of the house (Edinger 1985). Yet, it is only when she is meat that she can be rescued. As long as she tries to be a Goddess, she is trapped. When she becomes nothing, she becomes capable of receiving the "Water of Life" (Grace).

Ereshkigal: The Shadow Sister

Ereshkigal is not merely a villain or a monster to be slain; she is the **Shadow**, the necessary and terrifying counterpart to Inanna's brilliance. In Jungian psychology, the Shadow consists of every trait, emotion, and instinct that the conscious ego has rejected to maintain its ideal image (Jung 1959). While Inanna embodies the sanitized, socially acceptable aspects of the feminine, such as light, fertility, and organized power, Ereshkigal embodies the raw, unwashed reality of existence: grief, rage, entropy, and the physical finality of death. She is the "dark sister" who holds the memories of loss that the Queen of Heaven refuses to carry. The "groan" Inanna hears at the start of the myth is the voice of this repressed psychic material. It is the symptom that disrupts the ego's perfect life. When we ignore our shadow, it does not disappear; it festers underground. It groans through the floorboards of our consciousness, manifesting as anxiety, chronic pain, or a heavy, leaden depression that defies all rational attempts to fix it (Hillman 1979).

The turning point of the entire myth lies in the specific interaction between the Kurgarra and Galatur, creatures made of dirt who exist below the sexual binary, and the grieving Queen of the Underworld. They do not try to cheer her up, offer advice, or fix her pain. Instead, they perform a radical act of **mirroring**. When she cries "Oh, my inside," they echo, "Oh, your inside." When she cries "Oh, my outside," they echo, "Oh, your outside." This simple, rhythmic validation is the essence of empathy and the secret to healing the Plutonic wound. You cannot "lighten" the darkness of Pluto with platitudes; you can only witness it. By sitting with the Shadow and acknowledging its pain without judgment, the dynamic shifts (Johnson 1991). The Shadow, previously a devourer, transforms into a giver. Because she is finally heard, Ereshkigal releases her grip. She gives the body back, proving that the way out of hell is not to fight the darkness, but to join it in its lament until the energy is spent.

The Exchange: The Price of Renewal

The ending of the myth is brutal. Inanna sacrifices her husband, Dumuzi. This signifies that the **Old King**, the old dominant attitude of the consciousness, must die for the New Queen to live. Dumuzi represents the part of us that wants to remain in the "eternal summer" of childhood, the part that refuses to mourn, the part that sits on the throne wearing borrowed robes while the soul is dying. He is trapped in what James Hollis calls the "Saturnian Shadow," completely identified with his social role and his power, cut off from his own inner life (Hollis 1994). He is the 'Company Man' who has sacrificed his instinctual vitality for the safety of the social order, a trade-off Freud identified as the fundamental source of civilized misery (Freud 1930). He has become what Alasdair MacIntyre calls 'The Manager'—a character type defined entirely by effectiveness rather than moral purpose, treating his own soul not as a sacred vessel, but as a resource to be optimized (MacIntyre 1981).

Because he refuses to descend voluntarily, as Inanna did, he is dragged down forcibly by the demons. This is the psychological law of Pluto: that which refuses to transform is taken by force. Pluto demands a death. To return from the underworld, we must leave something behind. We cannot keep our old habits, our old dependencies, or our old naivety. We trade the "husband", the comfortable status quo, for the "soul", the integrated self.

Integration Practice: The Seven Gates of Attachment

Ask yourself: Who would you be if you lost what defines you?

- **Visualize the Descent:** Close your eyes and imagine standing at the First Gate.
- **Gate 1 (Status):** Imagine handing over your job title, your degree, your reputation. Who are you without them?
- **Gate 2 (Voice):** Imagine handing over your ability to explain yourself, to be "right," to be understood. Can you exist in silence?
- **Gate 3 (Possessions):** Imagine handing over your house, your car, your bank account.
- **Gate 4 (Relationships):** Imagine handing over the role of "partner," "parent," or "child." If you are not needed by anyone, do you still exist?
- **Gate 5 (Agency):** Imagine handing over your ability to fix things.
- **Gate 6 (Sexuality/Image):** Imagine handing over your physical beauty, your fitness, your attractiveness.
- **Gate 7 (The Self):** Imagine handing over your very name.
- **Practice:** You are now the meat on the hook. Just breathe. Feel the freedom of being nothing. From this place of zero, what is the one thing that actually wants to live? That is your Seed. That is what will survive the winter.

IV. References

- **Brinton Perera, S.** (1981). *Descent to the Goddess: A Way of Initiation for Women.* Toronto: Inner City Books.
- **Campbell, J.** (1949). *The Hero with a Thousand Faces.* New York: Pantheon Books.
- **Edinger, E.** (1985). *Anatomy of the Psyche: Alchemical Symbolism in Psychotherapy.* La Salle: Open Court.
- **Freud, S.** (1930). *Civilization and Its Discontents.* (J. Strachey, Trans.). London: The Hogarth Press.
- **Hillman, J.** (1979). *The Dream and the Underworld.* New York: Harper & Row.
- **Hollis, J.** (1994). *Under Saturn's Shadow: The Wounding and Healing of Men.* Toronto: Inner City Books.
- **Hollis, J.** (1996). *Swamplands of the Soul: New Life in Dismal Places.* Toronto: Inner City Books.
- **Hook, D.** (2017). *Six Moments in Lacan.* London: Routledge.
- **Johnson, R. A.** (1991). *Owning Your Own Shadow: Understanding the Dark Side of the Psyche.* San Francisco: HarperSanFrancisco.
- **Jung, C. G.** (1959). *The Archetypes and the Collective Unconscious* (Collected Works of C.G. Jung, Vol. 9, Part 1). Princeton: Princeton University Press.
- **MacIntyre, A. (1981).** *After Virtue: A Study in Moral Theory.* Notre Dame, IN: University of Notre Dame Press.
- **Meador, B. D.** (2000). *Inanna, Lady of Largest Heart: Poems of the Sumerian High Priestess Enheduanna.* Austin: University of Texas Press.
- **Wolkstein, D., & Kramer, S. N.** (1983). *Inanna, Queen of Heaven and Earth: Her Stories and Hymns from Sumer.* New York: Harper & Row.

11 EARTH: THE MOTHER AND REALITY

Archetype: The Great Mother, Substance, Incarnation, The Body
Myth: The Smith and the Devil (Proto-Indo-European / Folklore)

I. The Context: The Weight of the Real

We have traveled through the solar system, from the blinding ego of the Sun to the dissolution of Neptune, from the electric rebellion of Uranus to the crushing weight of Saturn. Now, at the end of our journey, we do not fly off into the cosmos. We fall. We return to the center of gravity that holds it all together. We return to Earth.

In astrological and alchemical traditions, Earth is rarely given its own chapter, often subsumed under the element of "matter" or divided among the signs of Taurus, Virgo, and Capricorn. But in this exploration, Earth is the final and most critical archetype. It is the principle of **Reality**. It is the *Unus Mundus* (One World) where the spirit must eventually land if it wishes to exist.

Earth is the realm of consequences. It is the realm of friction, of resistance, and of the body. It is where the infinite possibilities of the Puer Aeternus (the eternal child who flies) collide with the hard surface of necessity. It is the Kabbalistic **Malchut**, where the divine emanations of the Sephirot finally condense into the "Kingdom" of concrete form, becoming the vessel that holds the light in the material world (Scholem 1991).

To understand this archetype, we turn to a story that is older than the Bible, older than the pyramids, and perhaps one of the oldest stories humanity has ever told. Comparative mythologists have traced the roots of "The Smith and the Devil" back to the Proto-Indo-European era, some six thousand years ago. While the version we recount here wears the later, Christianized garb of medieval Europe, featuring St. Peter and the Devil, the underlying structure is primordial (Thompson 1955). We choose this familiar guise not for theological accuracy, but because it perfectly dramatizes the collision between the ego's craft and the absolute moral binaries it seeks to transcend. It is the story of the **Blacksmith**, the master of matter, the one who does not pray to the gods for deliverance but uses his own skill (*Technê*) to bind the chaotic forces of the underworld (Simpson 2009). It is a story about how we hammer out a soul in the heat of a material life.

II. The Myth

I invite you to locate the absolute center of your gravity. Find the heaviest part of your body. Feel the dense, calcium-rich reality of the bones in your legs, the solid mass of your pelvis resting against the chair, the pull of the planet beneath the floorboards claiming you as its own. Let your awareness drop out of your head, sliding down the spine, past the heart, past the gut, until it settles in the root. You are no longer floating in the ocean of Neptune or flying in the air of Uranus. You are on the ground. The air here is not thin or ethereal. It is thick, particulate, and heavy. It smells of things that burn and things that grow. It smells of coal dust, hot iron, and old sweat.

Let your inner eye open onto a landscape of hard, unyielding reality. It is the Iron Age. The world is stripped of color, painted in shades of gray, brown, and slate. It is a place of mud that sucks at the boots and stone that breaks the plow. In the center of a small, forgotten village stands a forge. It is a dark, squat building, hunkered down against the wind, its chimney belching thick, black smoke into the pale sky like a signal fire of industry. Inside, the heat is a physical presence. It presses against your skin like a heavy, suffocating blanket, drying the moisture from your eyes. The air tastes of sulfur and ash. The only light comes from the fire in the hearth, a roaring, angry orange eye that never blinks, casting long, dancing shadows against walls stained with centuries of soot.

At the anvil stands the Smith. Look at him. He is not a beautiful youth like Eros. He is not a radiant king like Oghuz. He is a man of the earth. His skin is leathered by the heat, stained permanently with soot. His hands are scarred, the fingers thick and calloused, shaped by the tools he holds. He is tired. He has worked this metal for forty years, beating the raw, resistant ore into plowshares and swords. He knows the secret of matter: it does not want to change. It resists. To shape the world, you must strike it, hard, repeatedly.

The Smith is poor, not with the romantic poverty of a monk, but with the grinding, humiliating poverty of a man who has failed to provide. His craft is noble, technically, but nobility does not put soup in the pot. The world outside his forge is cruel and indifferent. Rain drips through the thatch of his roof, a rhythmic, maddening torture that marks time in drops of cold water on the mud floor. Plink. Plink. Plink. It is the sound of his own inadequacy. His children are hungry. He sees it in the hollowness of their cheeks, in the way their eyes have grown too large for their faces, watching him with a silent, terrifying trust that he will fix it. But he cannot fix it. He has spent his life mastering the fire, coaxing potential out of the stubborn earth, yet he has nothing to show for it but a back that spasms with every breath and a pile of debts that grows like a tumor. He looks at the cold iron resting on his anvil. It is heavy, inert, and unresponsive. A bitterness rises in his throat, tasting of bile and ash. It is the specific, corrosive bitterness of the materialist who feels betrayed by the very matter he serves, the rage of a man who has given his body to the earth and received only stone in return.

One night, the rhythm of the forge is broken. It is not by a sound, but by a silence. The wind outside, which usually howls through the cracks in the walls, suddenly stops. The crickets in the grass cease their song. The air inside the forge grows heavy and still, charged with a static electricity that makes the hair on the Smith's arms stand up. It is the silence of a vacuum waiting to be filled.

Then, the door opens. There is no knock. There is no polite request for entry. The latch simply lifts, and the heavy oak door swings inward on silent hinges. A draft of air enters with the visitor, but it is not the cold night air of the village. It is a dry, scorching wind that smells of ancient dust and ozone. The fire in the hearth reacts instantly. It flares up, roaring in the chimney, but the color shifts. The comforting, familiar orange of burning wood bleeds away, replaced by a sickly, sulfurous green that casts long, unnatural shadows against the soot-stained walls.

A stranger stands on the threshold. He is tall, impossibly tall, ducking his head to enter the low room. He is dressed not in the rough wool of the peasantry, but in black velvet so deep and rich it seems to drink the light from the room, leaving a void where his body should be. He wears the face of a gentleman, handsome, refined, with a neatly trimmed beard, but the skin is too smooth, too pale, like wax that has never seen the sun.

But it is his eyes that betray him. They are not the eyes of a man who lives in time. They are old. They are older than the iron in the earth, older than the coal in the fire. They are vast, dark pools of intelligence that hold no warmth, only a terrifying, predatory patience. He leans against the doorframe with a casual elegance that feels mocking in this place of sweat and labor. He does not speak immediately. He simply watches the Smith work, his gaze heavy as lead, weighing the soul of the man before him.

"You labor hard," the stranger says. His voice is smooth, like oil sliding over polished stone.

"I labor," the Smith grunts, not looking up. "That is the lot of men."

"It does not have to be," the stranger replies. "I have watched you. You have the fire in your hands. You have the will. But you lack the power. I can give it to you."

The Smith stops his hammering. He wipes the sweat from his brow with a dirty rag. He looks at the stranger. He knows who this is. He does not need a name. This is the Adversary. The Shadow. The one who offers shortcuts through reality.

"What is the price?" the Smith asks. He is a practical man. He deals in trade.

"Your soul," the stranger says simply. "I will give you seven years of absolute power. Your skill will allow you to forge anything you can imagine. You will be the greatest craftsman the world has ever known. Wealth, fame, mastery. All yours. And at the end of seven years, you come with me."

The Smith looks at his cold anvil. It sits there, a mute block of iron that has demanded the strength of his youth and returned only an ache in his bones. He looks at the empty pot by the fire. It is a vessel of silence, a black hole that swallows his labor without ever being filled, a testament to the fact that his best efforts cannot fill the bellies of those he loves. He thinks of the years of struggle. He remembers the cold winters where the only warmth was the memory of summer, and the grinding poverty that eats at his dignity like rust devouring a blade. He looks at his own hands. They are scarred maps of his suffering, shaped by a lifetime of striking objects that refuse to yield.

He makes a calculation. It is not a moral weighing of good against evil. It is a structural assessment of load and resistance. He weighs the abstract promise of an eternal soul against the concrete reality of seven years of absolute agency. He asks himself if a soul that has known only hunger is worth saving. He decides that it is not. He decides that seven years of mastery, of imposing his will upon the stubborn earth, is better than a lifetime of slavery to the mud. He decides he would rather be the hammer for a moment than remain the anvil forever. He holds out his calloused hand.

"Done," he says.

The stranger smiles. He shakes the Smith's hand. The skin of the stranger is cold, burning cold, like iron left out in the winter frost. "Seven years," he whispers. "I will return."

The stranger vanishes. The fire returns to its normal color.

The change is immediate. The Smith picks up his hammer, and for the first time in forty years, it has no weight. It feels light as a feather, an extension of his own will rather than a burden. He strikes the iron. There is no resistance. The metal, usually stubborn and unyielding, moves like wet clay under his touch. It flows. He does not just shape it; he commands it. He discovers a geometry in his mind that he never learned, angles and curves that defy the limitations of the material.

He begins to forge. He makes swords with edges so keen they can cut a hair floating in the air, blades that can slice through stone as if it were cheese. He fashions plows that seem to possess their own hunger for the earth, tilling the soil without the need for oxen, turning the rocky fields into gardens. He moves to precious metals, spinning gold and silver into intricate, impossible filigrees that look like frozen lace or spiderwebs caught in the morning dew. The objects he creates vibrate with a strange, undeniable power. They are not just tools; they are artifacts of perfection.

The world notices. Word spreads from the village to the towns, and from the towns to the capital. The path to his door, once overgrown with weeds, is beaten flat by the feet of pilgrims. Kings send their messengers with chests of gold. Merchants travel from the east to buy his wonders. He becomes rich beyond the dreams of his ancestors. He tears down the leaking shack and builds a mansion of stone and oak. He fills his larder with meat and wine. He watches his children grow fat and strong, their cheeks rosy, the fear gone from their eyes. He has conquered the material world. He has bent reality to his desires.

But the Smith does not forget. He is a man of the earth, and he knows that debts must be paid. He does not spend the seven years in idleness. He spends them thinking. He studies the nature of binding. He studies the physics of the trap. He uses his supernatural skill not just to make beautiful things, but to forge a defense.

He decides to make a chair. To the eye, it is inviting. It is a wide, high-backed armchair upholstered in red velvet as plush as a king's robe. It looks like a place of rest, a throne of comfort for weary bones. But underneath the softness lies a skeleton of black iron, forged in the dead of a moonless night. As the Smith hammers the frame, he does not sing songs of praise. He chants spells of binding, low, guttural words that vibrate in the metal, locking the atoms into a pattern of unbreakable stasis. He carves runes of entrapment into the legs, hidden beneath the wood veneer, symbols that act like magnets for spiritual energy. Finally, he tempers the iron not in water, but in a mixture of holy water stolen from the church and the blood of a toad found in the graveyard. The liquid hisses with a sound like a thousand snakes. It is a masterpiece of deception, a prison disguised as a throne.

He creates an apple tree in his garden. It is beautiful, heavy with fruit, but he grafts the bark with lead and iron, twisting the roots into a knot that defies geometry. He whispers to the sap.

Seven years pass. To the day. To the hour.

The Smith stands at his anvil, though the hammer rests silent in his hand. He is waiting. The fire in the hearth has burned down to a bed of sullen, red coals, casting a dim, dying light across the soot-stained walls. He counts the beats of his own heart, measuring the final seconds of the contract. He knows the hour. He feels the weight of the years settling on his shoulders, a physical pressure that has nothing to do with gravity.

Then, the latch lifts. It is a slow, deliberate sound, metal scraping against metal in the quiet room. The heavy oak door swings inward, pushing a wedge of cold night air into the sweltering heat of the forge. The stranger enters. He steps across the threshold with the silence of a shadow detaching itself from a wall. He looks exactly as he did seven years ago. Time has flowed around him like water around a stone, leaving no mark, no wrinkle, no gray hair to mark the passage of the seasons. His black velvet coat is pristine, drinking the dim light. In his left hand, he holds a black sack. It hangs heavy, limp, and empty, a void waiting to be filled with the essence of a man.

"It is time," the stranger says. "You have had your glory. Now you belong to me."

The Smith puts down his hammer. He nods respectfully. "I know," he says. "I am a man of my word. I will come. But before we go, allow me one last courtesy. I have been working all day. My bones are old. Let me wash my hands and face so I do not enter your kingdom looking like a beggar."

The stranger, amused by this display of pride, nods. "Very well. Be quick."

"Please," the Smith says, gesturing to the iron chair in the corner. "Sit down. Rest your legs. It is a long journey to hell."

The stranger sits. He does not hesitate. He lowers his tall frame into the red velvet armchair with a sigh of anticipated luxury, the plush fabric yielding to his weight like a lover's embrace. He crosses his long legs, settling back against the cushions, and begins to look around the forge with a possessive air. His eyes scan the tools, the anvil, the cold fire, not as a guest, but as an owner surveying a foreclosure. He traces the lines of the hammers he gave power to, smiling a thin, cruel smile. He believes he has won. He believes the game is over.

The Smith turns his back on his guest. He walks to the stone basin in the corner of the room, his movements slow and deliberate. He dips his hands into the cold, black water. He begins to scrub. He washes away the soot of seven years. He scrubs the grease from under his fingernails, the charcoal dust from his knuckles. It is a ritual cleansing. The sound of the water splashing is loud in the silence. Splash. Drip. Splash. It is the sound of a man washing a corpse, or perhaps a man preparing for war.

He dries his hands on a rough cloth, taking his time, ensuring every drop of moisture is gone. Then, he puts on his heavy leather coat, buttoning it with a maddening slowness. Finally, he turns to the rack of tools. His eyes pass over the delicate hammers used for gold, the precision tools used for silver. He reaches past them. He reaches for the sledge. It is a block of solid iron on a hickory handle, a tool so heavy that no other man in the village can lift it. The handle is smooth, polished by the sweat of his life. He grips it. He lifts it. It feels light to him, charged with the power he bought with his soul.

He walks over to the chair. "Shall we go?" he asks.

The stranger tries to stand. He cannot. He frowns. He pushes against the arms of the chair. His hands are stuck. His back is stuck. His legs are fused to the seat. The velvet has become adhesive, stronger than glue, stronger than gravity. The iron of the chair seems to have grown into his flesh.

"What is this?" the stranger hisses. His eyes begin to glow with red fire. He summons his power. He tries to shapeshift, to turn into smoke, into a snake, into fire. But the chair holds him. It is a masterpiece of Techné, a trap built by human hands that overrides supernatural power.

"It is a chair," the Smith says calmly. "And you are sitting in it."

Then, the Smith raises the hammer. He does not pray. He does not ask for forgiveness. He swings. It is not a blow of anger, but of industry. He brings the iron sledge down on the stranger's toes. There is a crunch of bone that sickens the air, a wet, snapping sound that signals the breaking of something fundamental.

The Devil screams. It is a sound that shatters the windows of the forge, a high, inhuman shriek that tears at the fabric of the night. But the Smith does not stop. He finds a rhythm. Clang. Crunch. Clang. He swings again, aiming for the shins, the knees, the hands that grip the velvet arms. He beats the Devil. He hammers him as he would hammer a piece of raw, stubborn iron that refuses to take a shape. He is forging the trauma. He is working the material of his own suffering. He hits him until the scream dies into a sob, until the stranger begs, until the arrogance is beaten out of him like slag from a bloom. He reduces the supernatural predator to a whimpering thing trapped in a chair, broken by the very tools he mocked.

"Let me go!" the stranger shrieks, his voice thin and desperate. "I will tear up the contract! I will give you seven more years! Just let me go!"

The Smith leans on his hammer, breathing hard. "Seven more years?" he asks. "And you leave me alone?"

"Yes! Yes! Just release me!"

The Smith speaks a word. The chair releases. The stranger falls to the floor, bruised, broken, and humiliated. He scrambles to his feet and flees the forge, limping, vanishing into the night.

Seven more years pass. The Smith continues his work. He grows older. He grows sharper.

The stranger returns. But this time, there is no silent entry. There is no arrogant stride across the threshold. The Devil has learned the cost of underestimation. He stands well back from the forge, his boots sinking into the soft loam of the garden path. He keeps the heavy oak door between himself and the interior, eyeing the dark opening of the workshop with the suspicion of a wolf that has been caught in a trap. He does not cross the boundary. He stays under the open sky, where there are no walls to constrict him, no furniture to bind him.

"Come out!" he calls. His voice is not the smooth oil of the first visit, nor the terrified shriek of the second. It is hard, flat, and impatient. It carries across the evening air like the crack of a whip. "Your time is up, Smith. I know your games now. I will not enter your house. I will not sit in your chairs. Come out and pay what you owe."

The Smith walks out. He looks frail. He is coughing. "You are right," he says. "I am ready. I am tired of this life. But look at that apple tree. It is the last thing I grew. The fruit is ripe. I would love one last taste of an apple from my own garden before I go to the place where nothing grows."

The stranger looks at the tree. The apples are not merely red. They glow with a deep, ruby incandescence that seems to hold the last light of the setting sun within their skins. They are perfect spheres of temptation, heavy with juice, promising a burst of sweetness that could make a man, or a demon, forget the bitterness of the world. They hang low, just out of reach, their scent drifting on the breeze, a perfume of sugar and life that bypasses the mind and speaks directly to the appetite. It is a visual and olfactory feast, a concentrated image of everything the barren underworld lacks.

"Get it yourself," he sneers.

"I cannot climb," the Smith says. "My back is broken from the work. You are young. You are powerful. Could you not reach up and pick one for a dying man?"

The devil's vanity is piqued. It seems a simple request, a trivial exertion for a being who can span dimensions. He looks at the apple, hanging heavy and red, a perfect sphere of desire that seems to pulsate with its own inner light. He reaches up, his long, pale fingers stretching toward the fruit. He jumps. It is an easy, athletic motion, a display of physical grace meant to mock the Smith's frailty. His hand closes around the rough wood of the branch, expecting to snap the fruit free.

But the moment his skin touches the bark, the trap springs. The wood does not feel like timber; it feels like muscle contracting. The bark, grafted with lead and iron, bites into his flesh with the cold, unyielding grip of a vice. He tries to pull away, but the tree responds with a speed that defies biology. The leaves, sharp as razors, wrap around his wrists, binding him with the strength of steel handcuffs. The branches twist and knot around his arms, pulling him upward. The tree bends, groaning with the strain of the metal within its core, lifting his feet off the ground. He hangs there, suspended in the air, a dark fly caught in a web of living iron, helpless against the gravity of the Smith's design.

The Smith walks back into the forge. He moves with the unhurried gait of a man who has all the time in the world. He goes to the hearth, where the coals are glowing with a white-hot intensity. He takes a long iron poker, thrusting it deep into the heart of the fire until the tip turns the color of a cherry, then a bright, angry orange. He tests the heat against his cheek, feeling the radiation. He smiles, a grim expression that does not reach his eyes.

"Shall we negotiate?" the Smith asks, stepping back into the garden.

He does not wait for an answer. He reaches up with the poker. He presses the glowing metal against the sole of the Devil's boot. Leather sizzles and curls. The heat travels through the material, biting into the flesh beneath. The Devil thrashes, swinging like a pendulum in the grip of the tree, but the branches only tighten their hold. The Smith is methodical. He prods the ribs. He singes the fine black velvet coat. The smell of burning sulfur and scorched vanity fills the garden, choking out the sweet scent of the apples. It is a reversal of hell. The tormentor has become the tormented, suspended between the earth he despises and the sky he cannot reach.

The Smith leans on the poker, watching the smoke rise. "I have a condition," he says quietly. "I do not want wealth. I do not want more time. I want to be left alone. I want you to look at my soul and find it distasteful. I want you to reject it."

He raises the poker again. The Devil shrieks, a sound of absolute defeat that cracks the stone of the garden wall. "I will never come for you again!" he screams, his voice breaking into a thousand shards of panic. "I do not want your soul! It is too hard! It is too heavy! It is made of iron and spite! Keep it! Just let me down!"

The Smith releases him. The Devil flees, terrified of the man who has no fear.

Years later, the Smith finally dies. It is not a dramatic death. It is the slow, quiet cooling of a fire that has consumed all its fuel. He lies in his bed, the heavy quilts pulled up to his chin, listening to the rain on the roof, the sound that once tormented him now a gentle lullaby. His breath rattles in his chest, a bellows with a leak, and then simply stops. The heart, that muscle of tireless pumping, finally rests. He slips out of his body as easily as a hand slipping out of a work glove. He stands up. He looks at his own corpse, frail and wasted, and feels no attachment. He turns to the wall where his tools hang. He takes his hammer. He takes his tongs. He packs them into his leather bag. A craftsman does not travel without his trade.

He walks up the long road. It is a steep, uphill path paved with clouds that feel suspiciously like cotton wool. The air smells of incense and perfection, a cloying sweetness that makes his nose twitch. He reaches the Pearly Gates. They are impressive, he admits, wrought of gold and pearl, but the hinges look a bit stiff. St. Peter stands there, holding a ledger that is thicker than an anvil. He looks down at the Smith, his expression one of mild, bureaucratic distaste.

"You?" Peter says, flipping through the pages. "We have a record of you. You consorted with the Devil. You used magic, not prayer. You were greedy for the things of the earth. You negotiated your own salvation instead of asking for grace. You cannot come in here. This is a place for the pure, not the clever."

The Smith nods. He does not argue. He does not beg. He looks at the perfect, static light of Heaven, and he realizes it would bore him in a week. "Fair enough," he says.

He turns and walks down the road. He goes all the way down to the Gates of Hell. He knocks on the black iron door. A small demon opens the viewing slit. He sees the Smith standing there with his hammer.

The demon peering through the grate turns a sickly shade of gray. He stumbles back, tripping over his own tail in a frenzy of recognition. He has heard the whispers in the dark. He has seen the limp in his master's step. He shrieks, a high, piercing sound of pure terror that echoes off the black iron walls. "It is him! The man with the hammer is here! Do not open the gate! He is not a soul to be tortured. He is a monster who tortures! He will wreck the engines of hell! He will bind the master again!"

From the deepest pit, far below the crust of the earth, a roar answers. It is the voice of the Adversary, but it carries a tremor of remembered pain. The Devil has felt the weight of that hammer. He has felt the bite of the apple tree. The mere proximity of the Smith sends a shockwave of panic through the entire infernal hierarchy. "Lock the door!" he screams, his voice cracking with a fear that has no place in hell. "Bar the gates! Weld them shut! Do not let that man set one foot inside my kingdom! Keep him out!"

The Smith stands outside. Heaven won't have him. Hell is afraid of him. He is rejected by the spirit and rejected by the void. He takes a piece of coal from his pocket. He lights it with a snap of his fingers. He places it inside a hollowed-out turnip (or a pumpkin) to shield it from the wind.

He turns back to the world. He has nowhere else to go. He belongs to the Earth. He wanders the spaces between, carrying his own light, the master of his own fate, the one who hammered out his own immortality on the anvil of reality.

III. The Reflection

The story of the Smith and the Devil is the ultimate myth of **Earth**. It is not a story of transcendence or escape. It is a story of **Immanence**. It teaches us that the solution to the human condition is not found in the heavens, nor in the surrender to the abyss, but in the masterful manipulation of the material world through skill and will.

The *Unus Mundus* and the Smith

In alchemy and the later philosophy of Carl Jung, the term *Unus Mundus* refers to the "One World", the underlying reality where spirit and matter are not separate, but two aspects of the same substance (Jung 1970). The Smith is the priest of this reality. He works with **Iron**. Iron is the metal of Mars (aggression) and Saturn (structure). It is the hardest, most resistant material. The Smith does not pray to the iron; he heats it and beats it. This represents the ego's capacity to confront the "hardness" of life (trauma, poverty, limitation) and transform it not by fleeing, but by applying heat (consciousness) and pressure (work). The Smith is the archetype of the **Creator** in the material sense. He is not the dreamer (Neptune) or the rebel (Uranus). He is the Builder. He acts as the master of fire who accelerates the work of nature, imposing form upon chaotic matter (Eliade 1978). One could argue that he forces the spirit to inhabit the form.

The Sinthome: Hammering out a Soul

From a Lacanian perspective, this myth provides a beautiful illustration of the concept of the **Sinthome**. In his late teaching (specifically Seminar XXIII on James Joyce), Lacan moved beyond the idea that the subject must be organized by the "Name-of-the-Father" (the Law/God/Symbolic Order). He suggested that when the standard Oedipal structure fails or is rejected, the subject can create their own "fourth ring" to tie the psyche together. This self-made knot is the Sinthome (Lacan 2005).

The Smith is a man abandoned by the Symbolic Order. He is poor, ignored by God, and desperate. The "Name-of-the-Father" has failed him. So, he makes a deal with the Real (the Devil). But crucially, he does not succumb to the Real. He uses his **Techné** (his art, his craft) to bind it.

- **The Chair** and **The Tree** are his Sinthomes. They are artifices, human-made structures, that successfully trap the chaotic, destructive enjoyment of the Devil.

- The act of "beating the Devil" is the act of hammering out a psychic structure that holds. He beats the trauma into a shape that serves him.

The Smith saves himself not by being "good" (St. Peter rejects him), but by being *skillful.* He creates a unique, individual solution to the problem of existence. He becomes a "Self-Made Soul."

Techné vs. The Miracle

The myth contrasts two forms of power: the **Miracle** (what the Devil offers) and **Techné** (what the Smith uses). The Devil offers magic: instant wealth, instant power. This is the temptation of the inflation we saw in the Jupiter chapter. The Smith uses *Techné* (craft). Even though the Devil gave him the power, the Smith uses his *knowledge* of binding, of metal, of grafting trees to win. This teaches us that we cannot rely on luck, grace, or "manifesting" to save us from the shadow. We must develop competence. We must have a skill. Whether it is writing, carpentry, coding, or gardening, the mastery of a craft gives the ego a weapon against the chaos of the unconscious (Sennett 2008). The Smith is never afraid because he has his hammer. His confidence comes from his capability.

The Master-Slave Dialectic: The Inversion of Power

The dynamic between the Smith and the Devil perfectly enacts the famous **Master-Slave Dialectic** described by G.W.F. Hegel in *The Phenomenology of*

Spirit. Initially, the Devil positions himself as the Master. By granting the Smith power in exchange for his soul, he believes he has secured ultimate subservience. He exists in a state of pure consumption and enjoyment; he does not work, he merely takes.

However, Hegel argues that the Master's position is a dead end. Because the Master does not engage with the material world, he becomes dependent on the Slave's labor to satisfy his desires. The Slave (the Smith), through the discipline of work (*Arbeit*) and the struggle with resistant matter, achieves self-consciousness and mastery over nature. He exteriorizes his will into the object (the chair, the tree). By acquiring knowledge that the Master lacks, the power dynamic inverts. When the Devil sits in the chair, he discovers that his domination was an illusion. He is revealed as the dependent one, trapped by the very material reality he thought he owned, while the Smith, through his labor, has achieved true freedom (Hegel 1977).

The Wanderer: The Left-Hand Path

The ending is profound. The Smith is denied Heaven (the realm of the Spirit) and Hell (the realm of the Depths). He is forced to remain on Earth. This is not a punishment; it is a statement of his nature. He has become an **Earthbound Spirit**. He has integrated the opposites to such a degree that he no longer fits in the binary of "Good" vs. "Evil." He exists in the *Tertium Quid* (the Third Thing), the reality of human experience.

This trajectory mirrors the **Left-Hand Path** in Western esotericism. Unlike the Right-Hand Path, which seeks dissolution of the self into the Divine (union), the Left-Hand Path seeks the separation and strengthening of the individual consciousness (isolate intelligence). The goal is not to merge with God, but to become an independent center of the universe. The Smith carrying his own light (the coal in the turnip) is the perfect symbol of the "Black Flame," an internal, self-sustained luminosity that owes nothing to the sun of heaven or the fires of hell (Flowers 1997). He is the fully individuated human being who stands their ground, unafraid of the dark because they have beaten the Devil and lived to tell the tale.

Integration Practice: The Anvil

Ask yourself: What is the "iron" in your life that you are refusing to hammer?

- **Identify the Resistance:** Look for the part of your life that feels hardest, coldest, and most unyielding. Is it your physical health? Your finances? A difficult skill you are trying to learn? This is your Iron.

- **The Refusal of Magic:** Notice if you are waiting for a "miracle" (the Devil/Luck) to fix it. Are you waiting to be saved?

- **The Hammer:** What creates the solution? It is the repetitive, boring, hot, heavy work of the hammer. It is showing up to the forge every day.

Practice: Choose one "impossible" or "heavy" task. Commit to "beating" it for 15 minutes a day. Do not ask for it to be easy. Ask for your arm to be strong. Visualize yourself as the Smith. When the difficulty arises (the Devil), do not run. Trap it in the chair of your discipline and hammer it until it yields.

IV. References

- **Eliade, M.** (1978). *The Forge and the Crucible: The Origins and Structures of Alchemy.* Chicago: University of Chicago Press.

- **Flowers, S. E.** (1997). *Lords of the Left-Hand Path: Forbidden Practices and Spiritual Heresies.* Rochester, VT: Inner Traditions.

- **Hegel, G.W.F.** (1977). *Phenomenology of Spirit.* (A.V. Miller, Trans.). Oxford: Oxford University Press.

- **Jung, C. G.** (1970). *Mysterium Coniunctionis* (Collected Works of C.G. Jung, Vol. 14). Princeton: Princeton University Press.

- **Lacan, J.** (2005). *The Seminar of Jacques Lacan, Book XXIII: The Sinthome.* (A.R. Price, Trans.). Cambridge: Polity Press.

- **Scholem, G.** (1991). *On the Mystical Shape of the Godhead: Basic Concepts in the Kabbalah.* New York: Schocken Books.

- **Sennett, R.** (2008). *The Craftsman.* New Haven: Yale University Press.

- **Simpson, J.** (2009). *The Folklore of the Blacksmith.* London: Folklore Society.

- **Thompson, S.** (1955). *Motif-Index of Folk-Literature.* Bloomington: Indiana University Press.

CONCLUSION

We have reached the end of the trajectory. We have traveled from the blinding, ego-centric fire of the Sun, the radiant center of self-importance, to the damp, dissolving depths of Neptune, where all boundaries are lost to the oceanic infinite. We have felt the electric shock of Uranus shattering our complacencies and endured the crushing, leaden weight of Saturn, the great teacher of limitation and time. We have descended into the psychological underworld with Inanna to reclaim the buried gold of Pluto, and finally, we have returned to the surface to hammer that transformative ore into a tangible reality on the anvil of Earth.

The journey we have undertaken is not merely a tour of the solar system, a survey of inanimate spheres drifting through the vacuum of space. It is a tour of the human soul. Every crater, every storm, and every orbit we have examined finds its precise corollary in the emotional and psychological architecture of our daily lives. By mapping the heavens, we have simultaneously mapped the hidden contours of our own interiority.

The central premise of this book has been the ancient hermetic maxim: *As above, so below.* The map of the sky is the map of the psyche. The planets are not distant balls of gas and rock that exert a magical influence over us from millions of miles away. They are mirrors. They are the external projections of the internal powers that structure our existence (Jung, 1975).

However, studying these archetypes in isolation creates a false impression, suggesting a neat sequence of experiences; a Tuesday for Mars, a Wednesday for Venus. But the reality of our inner life is not sequential; it is simultaneous. We do not live in discrete modes; we live in the cacophony of all of them, all the time. The human psyche is not a serene monarchy ruled by a single, rational ego that calmly dictates policy. It is a turbulent oligarchy, a polytheistic pantheon composed of noisy, argumentative gods, where every seat is filled by a deity demanding their due, often at the exact same moment.

Consider the internal contradiction of a single hour: Mars demands we draw a sword and cut ties with a toxic situation, screaming for conflict and separation. Simultaneously, Venus whispers for reconciliation, urging us to smooth over the rough edges and find harmony at any cost. Saturn insists on building a fortress of security, hoarding resources and establishing boundaries to keep the world out. Yet, Jupiter, sitting right beside him, laughs at such caution, urging us to tear down the walls, take a massive risk, and expand into the unknown. Neptune offers the sweet, narcotic lure of dissociation and sleep, wishing to dissolve all problems into a mist, while Uranus acts as the electric alarm clock, shocking us into a state of hyper-awareness and demanding radical change now. This is not a linear progression; it is a riot.

The goal of this work, and the goal of the psychological life, is not to silence these voices. That leads to neurosis, the gray desert we saw in the chapter on Pluto. The goal is to integrate them and conduct them. The goal is to take the discordant shouts of the warring gods and weave them into a single, complex harmony.

Jung described this integration as individuation, a process of making the conscious ego permeable to the wisdom of the unconscious (Jung, 1966). Lacan, from a different vantage point, might describe it as softening the Symbolic order (the rigid Law of social structure) to acknowledge the vital, often disruptive desires of the Imaginary (Fink, 1995). Yet, whichever map of the mind you prefer, the territory reveals the same inescapable truth: that which is repressed refuses to be silenced. It does not disappear; it goes underground. And as we have seen throughout these chapters, that which you push down will eventually return with a vengeance.

To visualize this final integration, we turn to one of the most profound visions in Western philosophy. We look to the end of Plato's *Republic*, to the story of a soldier named Er. It is a myth about the structure of the cosmos, the necessity of choice, and the sound that the universe makes when all its parts are moving together. It is the myth of the Music of the Spheres.

In his vision, Er bears witness to the machinery of existence, seeing the cosmos bound together by the Spindle of Necessity. This is not a passive structure, but a dynamic, cosmic loom presided over by the goddess Ananke, the personification of inevitability. At its center stands a vast, spinning shaft of light, described as a pillar stretching through heaven and earth, brilliant as a rainbow but searingly distinct. This shaft acts as the immutable axis of the universe, the unshakeable pole around which all life revolves. Turning around this spindle are eight concentric whorls, fitted into one another like a set of nested bowls, their rims forming a continuous flat surface while their depths vary. These represent the orbits of the planets, moving in their inexorable tracks: from the heavy, slow-moving outer spheres to the swift inner circuits, each distinct in color and velocity, yet all bound to the same central turning force.

Plato tells us that on the rim of each whorl stands a Siren. As the orbit spins, the Siren utters a single sound, one distinct tone. Alone, the note is monotonous. But because the whorls are spinning at different speeds, and the Sirens are singing together, the notes blend to create a single, perfect harmony. This is the celestial music. It is the sound of the universe in order.

Sitting around the spindle are the three Fates, the daughters of Necessity. They are dressed in white robes, chanting to the music of the Sirens: Lachesis sings of the past, Clotho of the present, and Atropos of the future. This trio finds its echo in the Norns of Scandinavian myth (Urd, Verdandi, and Skuld) who weave the destinies of gods and men alike at the foot of the World Tree.

This is the final image I wish to leave you with, not as a model of the heavens, but as a model of yourself.

Whether you perceive life as a woven tapestry or a musical composition, the central truth remains: you are the Spindle of Necessity, the trunk of your own World Tree. You are the axis upon which your own universe turns. The planets we have studied are the whorls spinning around your center.

If one of these whorls is stuck, or spinning out of control, the music becomes a discord. If you suppress your Mars, the bass note of your vitality vanishes, and the melody becomes thin and fragile. If you refuse the boundaries of Saturn, the rhythm collapses into chaos. The "good life" is not found in the purity of silence, but in the richness of the chord.

The work of individuation, then, is the work of a composer. It requires the wisdom to know when to let the brass section of Mars roar, and when to bring it to a hush so the delicate strings of Venus can be heard. It requires the patience of Saturn to learn the scales, and the daring of Uranus to improvise.

In the myth, before the souls return to Earth to be born, they appear before Lachesis to choose their lots in life. They are not assigned a destiny; they choose one. This implies that while the archetypes are universal, the way we embody them is a choice. We do not choose the planets (everyone is born with a Mars, a Moon, and a Saturn) but we choose how to play them.

When you look up at the night sky, you are not looking at foreign territory. You are looking at a reflection of your own interiority. The gods are not out there; they are in here. They are waiting for you to pick up the baton.

The symphony has already begun. It is playing in your desires, your fears, your dreams, and your daily acts of creation. It is time to stop covering your ears to the noise, and start conducting the music. As Gustav Mahler famously said:

> "The symphony must be like the world. It must embrace everything."

I. References

- **Fink, B.** (1995). *The Lacanian Subject: Between Language and Jouissance.* Princeton University Press.

- **Jung, C. G.** (1966). *Two Essays on Analytical Psychology* (R. F. C. Hull, Trans.). Princeton University Press. (Original work published 1928)

- **Jung, C. G.** (1975). Letter to André Barbault, 26 May 1954. In G. Adler & A. Jaffé (Eds.), *C.G. Jung Letters: Vol. 2, 1951-1961.* Princeton University Press.

GLOSSARY

Anima (Jungian) The inner feminine personality in the unconscious of a man. In this book, it is explored not just as a gendered concept, but as the archetype of *Zoé* (indestructible life) and the force of connection to the unconscious. It is the "Soul Image" that leads the ego into the deeper layers of the psyche.

Animus (Jungian) The inner masculine personality in the unconscious of a woman. While the Anima connects a man to the soul (*Eros*), the Animus connects a woman to the spirit (*Logos*). It represents the capacity for focus, discrimination, and conviction. When unconscious, it can manifest as rigid opinions or aggressive argumentation ("the sword used clumsily"), but when integrated, it becomes a source of intellectual clarity, creative power, and the courage to act.

Archetype (Jungian) Universal, archaic patterns and images that derive from the collective unconscious and are the psychic counterpart of instinct. They are the inherited "organs" of the psyche (e.g., The Hero, The Mother, The Trickster) that shape our perception and behavior.

Axis Mundi (Mythological) The "Center of the World" or the cosmic connection between Heaven and Earth. Psychologically, it represents the central organizing principle of the Self that grounds the personality and provides stability amidst chaos.

Collective Unconscious (Jungian) The deepest layer of the psyche, shared by all human beings. It contains the archetypes and the accumulated heritage of human evolution, distinct from the personal unconscious which contains individual memories and repressions.

Drive (Trieb) (Lacanian/Freudian) Often confused with biological instinct, the Drive is something purely psychological and much stranger. While an instinct has a clear goal (hunger leads to eating, which leads to satisfaction), the Drive is a constant, circulating energy that never actually wants to reach its goal. It enjoys the *process* of circling. Think of it as a "zombie" energy inside us that persists beyond logic and biological need, constantly pushing us to repeat certain behaviors.

Ego (Jungian) The center of the conscious field. The "I" that organizes reality, perceives identity, and maintains continuity in time. It is represented by the Sun.

Imaginary, The (Lacanian) One of the three orders of the psyche (along with the Symbolic and the Real). This is the realm of images, mirrors, and appearances. It is where we say "That's me!" when looking in a mirror or at a photo. However, it is fundamentally deceptive because it is based on surface wholeness. In the Imaginary, we believe we are whole, consistent, and beautiful, ignoring the internal cracks and conflicts. It is the filter of "fantasy" we place over the world.

Individuation (Jungian) The lifelong psychological process of differentiation and integration. It involves separating from the collective norms and integrating the unconscious aspects of the self (Shadow, Anima/Animus) to become a unique, whole individual ("The Self").

Inflation (Jungian) A state where the ego identifies with an archetype (e.g., believing one *is* the King or the Savior). It results in a loss of reality and a dangerous expansion of the personality, often followed by a collapse.

Jouissance (Lacanian) A French term that translates to "enjoyment," but in psychoanalysis, it means something much more intense. While "pleasure" is comfortable and keeps us safe (like a warm bath), *Jouissance* is an excess of life that can be painful or destructive (like scratching an itch until it bleeds, or the thrill of a roller coaster). It is the kind of intense excitement that the body can barely handle, lying on the border between ecstasy and suffering.

Mana Personality (Jungian) A personality that has become charged with "mana" (magical or spiritual power) after integrating contents from the unconscious. While powerful, it carries the risk of inflation if the ego believes the power belongs to it personally rather than to the archetype.

Master Signifier (S_1) (Lacanian) A word or symbol that holds a belief system together. It doesn't necessarily have a clear definition, but it stops us from questioning things. Examples include "God," "The Nation," "Freedom," or even a parent's "Because I said so." It acts like the quilting button on a sofa: it pins down the fabric of reality so that everything stays in place and makes sense.

Mirror Stage (Lacanian) A critical developmental moment (usually between 6 and 18 months) when an infant recognizes their reflection in a mirror. Before this, the baby feels like a fragmented bundle of limbs and sensations. Seeing the image, they think, "That whole, perfect thing is me!" This creates the Ego, but it also creates a lifelong problem: we forever identify with an external image rather than our internal reality.

Name-of-the-Father (Nom-du-Père) (Lacanian) This doesn't necessarily refer to your biological dad. It refers to the function of "The Law" or authority that separates a child from their mother. It is the metaphorical "No" that breaks the cozy, silent bond of infancy and forces us to use language to ask for what we want. It is the entrance fee we pay to become members of society.

Negative Senex (Jungian) The shadow side of the Wise Old Man archetype (Saturn). It manifests as rigidity, bitterness, resistance to change, and the devouring of the new (eating the children) to maintain the status quo.

Nigredo (Alchemical) The "Blackening." The first stage of the alchemical opus, associated with Saturn and lead. Psychologically, it represents depression, decomposition, and the breakdown of the old ego structures necessary for transformation.

Objet petit a (Lacanian) The "object cause of desire." Imagine a donkey chasing a carrot on a stick. The donkey thinks it wants the carrot, but what actually drives the donkey is the *distance* of the carrot. *Objet petit a* is that missing piece, that "little something" we feel is always missing. It is not a specific object (like a new phone or a lover), but the void *behind* those objects that keeps us desiring. It is the engine of human longing.

Oceanic Feeling (Freudian) A sensation of limitless connection to the universe, a return to the state of primary narcissism before the ego separated from the world. In this book, it is associated with Neptune and the urge to dissolve.

Persona (Jungian) The social mask the ego wears to interact with the world. It is necessary for social functioning but becomes dangerous if the individual identifies with it completely, forgetting their true nature.

Puer Aeternus (Jungian) Latin for "Eternal Boy." An archetype associated with high creativity, spirituality, and idealism, but also with a refusal to grow up, commit to earth, or accept the limitations of time and reality.

Quilting Point (Point de Capiton) (Lacanian) In upholstery, a quilting point is the button that holds the stuffing and the fabric together so the shape is maintained. In the psyche, language is a fluid, sliding chain of words (signifiers) that can mean anything. A Quilting Point is a specific anchor—like a core belief, a Master Signifier, or a trauma—that stops this sliding and pins meaning down. It creates stability. Without these points, our reality would be a chaotic flux (psychosis).

Real, The (Lacanian) The most difficult concept to grasp. The Real is *not* "reality" (which is the world we understand). The Real is the raw, unnamable trauma of existence that cannot be put into words. It is the car crash before you can describe it; it is the sudden death; it is the sheer chaos of nature. It is the "hard kernel" of life that resists all our attempts to make sense of it.

Self, The (Jungian) The archetype of wholeness and the regulating center of the psyche. It encompasses both the conscious ego and the unconscious. It is the goal of individuation, often represented by the mandala, the stone, or the divine child.

Shadow (Jungian) The unconscious aspect of the personality which the conscious ego does not identify in itself. It contains rejected traits (weaknesses, aggression, desires) that are incompatible with the Persona. Amongst these rejected traits, rich sources of strength, vitality and creativity can often be found.

Signifier (Lacanian/Linguistic) Simply put, a "sound-image" or a word (like the word "Tree"). Lacan argues that our unconscious is a web of these words. The important thing to know is that a signifier doesn't point to a real object; it points to *other* signifiers. (e.g., If you look up "Tree" in a dictionary, you get more words). We are trapped in this web of language, which shapes how we experience the world.

Sinthome (Lacanian) When the standard rules of society (the Name-of-the-Father) fail to hold a person together, they can fall apart (psychosis). A *Sinthome* is a self-made knot that ties the psyche back together. It is often a unique creative practice, a specific obsession, or a craft (like the Smith's forging or James Joyce's writing) that allows a person to function and survive despite their internal chaos.

Subjective Destitution (Lacanian) A state often reached at the end of deep psychological work or a major life crisis. It is the moment you realize that all your titles—"Boss," "Mother," "Good Person"—are just empty badges. You are reduced to zero. While this sounds terrifying, it is the moment of ultimate freedom, where you stop living for the approval of others and exist as you truly are.

Symbolic Order, The (Lacanian) The world of rules, language, laws, and social contracts. It is the "Matrix" we live in. From the moment we are given a name, we enter the Symbolic Order. It allows us to communicate and live together, but it alienates us from our raw, animal nature.

Synchronicity (Jungian) An "acausal connecting principle." The meaningful coincidence of an inner psychological state (e.g., a dream) with an external event, suggesting a connection between the psyche and the material world.

Techné (Greek) Art, craft, or skill. In this book, it refers to the ego's ability to manipulate matter and bind the chaotic forces of the unconscious through disciplined work and creation.

Trickster (Jungian) An archetypal figure (like Mercury) who crosses boundaries, breaks rules, and disrupts the established order. The Trickster embodies the chaos and creativity of the pre-conscious mind.

Unus Mundus (Alchemical) Latin for "One World." The concept of an underlying unitary reality where matter and psyche are not separate but two aspects of the same substance.

BIBLIOGRAPHY

Aeschylus. (2009). *Prometheus Bound.* (J. Scully & C.J. Herington, Trans.). Oxford: Oxford University Press.

Apuleius, L. (1996). *The Golden Ass.* (P.G. Walsh, Trans.). Oxford: Oxford University Press.

Assmann, J. (2001). *The Search for God in Ancient Egypt.* (D. Lorton, Trans.). Ithaca: Cornell University Press.

Bacigalupo, A. M. (2007). *Shamans of the Foye Tree: Gender, Power, and Healing among the Chilean Mapuche.* Austin: University of Texas Press.

Bachelard, G. (1969). *The Poetics of Space.* (M. Jolas, Trans.). Boston: Beacon Press.

Bataille, G. (1986). *Erotism: Death and Sensuality.* San Francisco: City Lights Books.

Bazin, L. (1991). *Les Systèmes chronologiques dans le monde turc ancien.* Budapest: Akadémiai Kiadó.

Bennis, W. G., & Thomas, R. J. (2002). "Crucibles of Leadership." *Harvard Business Review*, 80(9), 39–45.

Bly, R. (1990). *Iron John: A Book About Men.* Reading, MA: Addison-Wesley.

Brinton Perera, S. (1981). *Descent to the Goddess: A Way of Initiation for Women.* Toronto: Inner City Books.

Campbell, J. (1949). *The Hero with a Thousand Faces*. New York: Pantheon Books.

Campbell, J. (1964). *The Masks of God: Occidental Mythology*. New York: Viking Press.

Cooper, J. M. (1946). "The Araucanians." In *Handbook of South American Indians, Vol. 2*. Washington: Government Printing Office.

Corbin, H. (1969). *Creative Imagination in the Sufism of Ibn 'Arabi*. (R. Manheim, Trans.). Princeton: Princeton University Press.

Crossley-Holland, K. (1980). *The Norse Myths*. New York: Pantheon Books.

Deleuze, G., & Guattari, F. (1983). *Anti-Oedipus: Capitalism and Schizophrenia*. (R. Hurley et al., Trans.). Minneapolis: University of Minnesota Press.

Diamond, S. A. (1996). *Anger, Madness, and the Daimonic: The Psychological Genesis of Violence, Evil, and Creativity*. Albany: SUNY Press.

Edinger, E. (1972). *Ego and Archetype: Individuation and the Religious Function of the Psyche*. New York: G.P. Putnam's Sons.

Edinger, E. (1985). *Anatomy of the Psyche: Alchemical Symbolism in Psychotherapy*. La Salle: Open Court.

Eliade, M. (1959). *The Sacred and the Profane: The Nature of Religion*. New York: Harcourt, Brace & World.

Eliade, M. (1978). *The Forge and the Crucible: The Origins and Structures of Alchemy*. Chicago: University of Chicago Press.

Estés, C. P. (1992). *Women Who Run with the Wolves: Myths and Stories of the Wild Woman Archetype*. New York: Ballantine Books.

Faron, L. C. (1964). *Hawks of the Sun: Mapuche Morality and Its Ritual Attributes*. Pittsburgh: University of Pittsburgh Press.

Faulkner, R. O. (1972). *The Ancient Egyptian Book of the Dead*. London: British Museum Press.

Fink, B. (1995). *The Lacanian Subject: Between Language and Jouissance*. Princeton: Princeton University Press.

Flowers, S. E. (1997). *Lords of the Left-Hand Path: Forbidden Practices and Spiritual Heresies*. Rochester, VT: Inner Traditions.

Frankl, V. E. (1959). *Man's Search for Meaning.* Boston: Beacon Press.

Freud, S. (1913). *Totem and Taboo: Resemblances Between the Psychic Lives of Savages and Neurotics.* (A. A. Brill, Trans.). New York: Moffat, Yard and Company.

Freud, S. (1920). *Beyond the Pleasure Principle.* (J. Strachey, Trans.). London: The Hogarth Press.

Freud, S. (1930). *Civilization and Its Discontents.* (J. Strachey, Trans.). London: The Hogarth Press.

Granholm, K. (2014). *Dark Enlightenment: The Historical, Sociological, and Discursive Contexts of Contemporary Esoteric Magic.* Leiden: Brill.

Graves, R. (1955). *The Greek Myths.* London: Penguin Books.

Greene, L. (1996). *The Astrological Neptune and the Quest for Redemption.* York Beach, ME: Samuel Weiser.

Greene, L. (2018). *Jung's Studies in Astrology: Prophecy, Magic, and the Qualities of Time.* London: Routledge.

Hand, R. (1976). *Planets in Transit: Life Cycles for Living.* Atglen, PA: Whitford Press.

Hegel, G.W.F. (1977). *Phenomenology of Spirit.* (A.V. Miller, Trans.). Oxford: Oxford University Press.

Herzog, E. (1998). *Psyche and Death.* Dallas: Spring Publications.

Hesiod. (2006). *Theogony.* (M.L. West, Trans.). Oxford: Oxford University Press.

Hillman, J. (1975). *Re-Visioning Psychology.* New York: Harper & Row.

Hillman, J. (1979). *The Dream and the Underworld.* New York: Harper & Row.

Hillman, J. (2005). *Senex and Puer: An Aspect of the Historical Present.* Putnam: Spring Publications.

Hollis, J. (1994). *Under Saturn's Shadow: The Wounding and Healing of Men.* Toronto: Inner City Books.

Hollis, J. (1996). *Swamplands of the Soul: New Life in Dismal Places.* Toronto: Inner City Books.

Hook, D. (2017). *Six Moments in Lacan.* London: Routledge.

Hornung, E. (1999). *The Ancient Egyptian Books of the Afterlife.* Ithaca: Cornell University Press.

Hulak, F. (2020). *Ce que Lacan nous enseigne.* Paris: Erès.

Johnson, R. A. (1991). *Owning Your Own Shadow: Understanding the Dark Side of the Psyche.* San Francisco: HarperSanFrancisco.

Jung, C. G. (1959). *The Archetypes and the Collective Unconscious* (Collected Works of C.G. Jung, Vol. 9, Part 1). Princeton: Princeton University Press.

Jung, C. G. (1960). *The Structure and Dynamics of the Psyche* (Collected Works of C.G. Jung, Vol. 8). Princeton: Princeton University Press.

Jung, C. G. (1964). *Man and His Symbols.* London: Aldus Books.

Jung, C. G. (1966). *Two Essays on Analytical Psychology* (Collected Works of C.G. Jung, Vol. 7). Princeton: Princeton University Press.

Jung, C. G. (1967). *Symbols of Transformation* (Collected Works of C.G. Jung, Vol. 5). Princeton: Princeton University Press.

Jung, C. G. (1968). *Psychology and Alchemy* (Collected Works of C.G. Jung, Vol. 12). Princeton: Princeton University Press.

Jung, C. G. (1969). *The Archetypes and the Collective Unconscious* (Collected Works of C.G. Jung, Vol. 9, Part 1). Princeton: Princeton University Press.

Jung, C. G. (1970). *Mysterium Coniunctionis* (Collected Works of C.G. Jung, Vol. 14). Princeton: Princeton University Press.

Jung, C. G. (1975). Letter to André Barbault, 26 May 1954. In G. Adler & A. Jaffé (Eds.), *C.G. Jung Letters: Vol. 2, 1951-1961.* Princeton: Princeton University Press.

Jung, C. G. (1982). *Aspects of the Feminine.* Princeton: Princeton University Press.

Jung, C. G. (2009). *The Red Book: Liber Novus.* (S. Shamdasani, Ed.). New York: W. W. Norton & Company.

Kalsched, D. (1996). *The Inner World of Trauma: Archetypal Defenses of the Personal Spirit.* London: Routledge.

Keene, D. (1967). *Japanese Literature: An Introduction for Western Readers.* New York: Grove Press.

Kerenyi, C. (1976). *Dionysos: Archetypal Image of Indestructible Life.* Princeton: Princeton University Press.

Kerenyi, C. (1997). *Prometheus: Archetypal Image of Human Existence.* Princeton: Princeton University Press.

Klages, L. (1929–32). *Der Geist als Widersacher der Seele* (3 vols.). Leipzig: Barth.

Klibansky, R., Panofsky, E., & Saxl, F. (1964). *Saturn and Melancholy: Studies in the History of Natural Philosophy, Religion, and Art.* London: Nelson.

Kripal, J. J. (2001). *Roads of Excess, Palaces of Wisdom: Eroticism and Reflexivity in the Study of Mysticism.* Chicago: University of Chicago Press.

Lacan, J. (1976). *The Seminar of Jacques Lacan, Book XXIII: The Sinthome.* (A.R. Price, Trans.). Cambridge: Polity Press.

Lacan, J. (1978). *The Four Fundamental Concepts of Psycho-Analysis* (Book XI). New York: W. W. Norton & Company.

Lacan, J. (1992). *The Seminar of Jacques Lacan, Book VII: The Ethics of Psychoanalysis 1959–1960.* (D. Porter, Trans.). New York: W. W. Norton & Company.

Lacan, J. (2006). *Écrits: The First Complete Edition in English.* (B. Fink, Trans.). New York: W. W. Norton & Company.

Lacan, J. (2007). *The Other Side of Psychoanalysis: The Seminar of Jacques Lacan, Book XVII.* (R. Grigg, Trans.). New York: W. W. Norton & Company.

Lacan, J. (2015). *Transference: The Seminar of Jacques Lacan, Book VIII.* (B. Fink, Trans.). Cambridge: Polity Press.

Lévi-Strauss, C. (1969). *The Raw and the Cooked: Introduction to a Science of Mythology.* New York: Harper & Row.

Lewis, G. (1974). *The Book of Dede Korkut.* London: Penguin Classics.

MacIntyre, A. (1981). *After Virtue: A Study in Moral Theory.* Notre Dame, IN: University of Notre Dame Press.

Meador, B. D. (2000). *Inanna, Lady of Largest Heart: Poems of the Sumerian High Priestess Enheduanna.* Austin: University of Texas Press.

Métraux, A. (1946). *Myths of the Toba and Pilagá Indians of the Gran Chaco.* Philadelphia: American Folklore Society.

Meza, G. (2025). *Neptune and the Object-Cause of Desire.* Retrieved from https://www.astro-rose.fr/en/journal

Moore, R., & Gillette, D. (1990). *King, Warrior, Magician, Lover: Rediscovering the Archetypes of the Mature Masculine.* San Francisco: HarperSanFrancisco.

Neumann, E. (1954). *The Origins and History of Consciousness.* Princeton: Princeton University Press.

Neumann, E. (1956). *Amor and Psyche: The Psychic Development of the Feminine.* Princeton: Princeton University Press.

Ögel, B. (1993). *Türk Mitolojisi (Kaynakları ve Açıklamaları ile Destanlar).* Ankara: Türk Tarih Kurumu Basımevi.

Richardson, M. (2016). *The Tale of the Bamboo Cutter.* [Translation and Commentary]. CreateSpace Independent Publishing Platform.

Scholem, G. (1991). *On the Mystical Shape of the Godhead: Basic Concepts in the Kabbalah.* New York: Schocken Books.

Sennett, R. (2008). *The Craftsman.* New Haven: Yale University Press.

Simpson, J. (2009). *The Folklore of the Blacksmith.* London: Folklore Society.

Sturluson, S. (2005). *The Prose Edda.* (J.L. Byock, Trans.). London: Penguin Classics.

Tarnas, R. (2006). *Cosmos and Psyche: Intimations of a New World View.* New York: Viking.

Te Velde, H. (1967). *Seth, God of Confusion: A Study of His Role in Egyptian Mythology and Religion.* Leiden: Brill.

Terán, B. (1994). *Lo que cuentan los wichís.* Buenos Aires: Ediciones del Sol.

Thomas, D. (2020). *The Deep Psychology of BDSM and Kink.* London: Routledge.

Thompson, S. (1955). *Motif-Index of Folk-Literature.* Bloomington: Indiana University Press.

Von Franz, M. L. (1972). *Problems of the Feminine in Fairytales.* Dallas: Spring

Publications.

Von Franz, M. L. (1980). *The Golden Ass of Apuleius: The Liberation of the Feminine in Man*. Boston: Shambhala.

Von Franz, M. L. (2000). *The Problem of the Puer Aeternus*. Toronto: Inner City Books.

Wilbert, J., & Simoneau, K. (1982). *Folk Literature of the Mataco Indians*. Los Angeles: UCLA Latin American Center Publications.

Wolkstein, D., & Kramer, S. N. (1983). *Inanna, Queen of Heaven and Earth: Her Stories and Hymns from Sumer*. New York: Harper & Row.

Woodman, M. (1982). *Addiction to Perfection: The Still Unravished Bride*. Toronto: Inner City Books.

Žižek, S. (1989). *The Sublime Object of Ideology*. London: Verso.

Žižek, S. (2006). *How to Read Lacan*. London: Granta Books.

ABOUT THE AUTHOR

Gonzalo Esteban Meza is a corporate leader, published author, and volunteer firefighter. An engineer by training with a lifelong passion for the human condition, he holds an MBA in Leadership and is currently pursuing an MSc in Psychology. This unique blend of technical rigor and psychological insight allows him to approach the complexities of the mind with both structure and empathy. Also a diving instructor, he brings a passion for exploration to his work, whether navigating the depths of the ocean or the intricacies of the human experience.

Together with his wife **Gülsah**, he works to guide individuals on their own journeys of individuation. Through their shared initiative, they combine their strengths to help others break free from their constraints, identify their own patterns, and reclaim their vitality.

United by a profound love for scuba diving, Gonzalo and Gülsah share a lively home with four rescue pets, all of whom labor under the charming illusion that they are the ones running the house.

You can contact them and learn more about their work via their company, **La Rose et l'Astre**, at www.astro-rose.fr.

OTHER BOOKS BY THE AUTHOR

Salt & Lightning

The Art of Being Uncomfortable: A Leadership Manifesto

Lilith, Volupté Insoumise (with Gülsah Meza)

The Star, the Shadow, and the Cosmic Mirror (with Gülsah Meza)

www.ingramcontent.com/pod-product-compliance
Lightning Source LLC
Chambersburg PA
CBHW050529240926
51846CB00003B/745
* 9 7 8 2 4 8 8 9 3 6 0 0 2 *